Who Made The Milk Police?

NICOLA SAUNDERS
THE PARENTING EXPERT

Who Made YOU The Milk Police?

PREVENT PARENTAL BURNOUT: 50 WAYS TO MASTER STRESS-FREE PARENTING

NICOLA SAUNDERS
THE PARENTING EXPERT

To my children and my mentor (and work mum), Glenda Melville

I wouldn't be who I am today without you. You've taught me more than I could have imagined, and each of you has enhanced my personal and professional growth in ways I'll forever be grateful for. I'm so thankful to have had you by my side through this incredible journey called life.

And to my husband

Thank you for being my rock, always standing by me with unwavering love and support. You're my greatest cheerleader and constant source of strength. I'm so grateful to walk through life with you by my side.

Contents

I'VE BEEN RIGHT WHERE YOU ARE

Show me a parent who hasn't felt like their brain might explode from the constant pressures of family and work life at some point. We've all been there. Not only have I been there, but I've also worked with many parents who feel the same way. Sadly, this is often not a one-off event, and in today's busy world, many parents are in a constant state of stress for numerous reasons.

WHAT IS BURNOUT?

Let's not sugar coat this, burnout is awful, it is like carrying an invisible load that gets heavier every day. It's that overwhelming feeling when every small task feels monumental, and you're constantly on edge. It's more than just being tired;

it's emotional exhaustion that makes even the things you once enjoyed feel like chores. When burnout hits, it leaves you feeling disconnected from yourself and those around you, like you're running on empty but still expected to keep going.

One of the first things we tend to stop doing when we become emotionally exhausted is the things that we love and actually refuel us. That may be exercise, hobbies, or reading a book, the logic being "I don't have the time for that right now," when in reality, those are the very things you need the most."

This book is your guide to avoiding that trap. Speaking from experience, I had no idea burnout was coming for me almost 17 years ago. It felt like it came out of nowhere. But looking back, the warning signs were all there. I just kept telling myself to push through until one day, I couldn't anymore. Burnout had caught up with me, even though nothing about that particular week was different from the 52 that came before it. And that's the point, it builds up quietly, slowly, until your body finally throws in the towel and demands rest.

I will never forget how burnout made me

feel. I felt exhausted and lost, my body ached like never before, and my brain just felt like mush. I was juggling being a mum and working until late into the evening around my family commitments and I was firing on all cylinders until one day, BOOM, my body and mind just stopped me in my tracks. It even made me question whether I could continue in my work as a therapist, a job I loved. But what I learned was that it wasn't the job that tipped me over the burnout edge; it was my mindset and how poorly I was taking care of myself. I was great at looking after everybody else, but I wasn't practising what I preached when it came to myself. I promised never to let myself get to that point again, and I've kept it.

Your emotional energy is the one thing that will keep you showing up with whatever hat you have on today, whether that be as a parent, partner, employee, employer or friend. Your emotional energy matters. So, let's get into what this all means.

Before We Start

Let me introduce you to your guide to creating your very own unique "Emotional First Aid Box." Throughout this book, I will give you many ideas about how to look after your overall emotional well-being, some of which you may already do, some you may be keen to try, and others that may make you feel a little uncomfortable, or you may even roll your eyes and think 'yeah yeah, I know all about that'. Please enter this with an open mind. How you look after your emotional well-being and take care of it when it feels a bit battered is really important. If you had a scratch on your arm, you're not likely to wrap it in a sling as it's not fit for purpose; that's what plasters are for. This is why we need various options in our Emotional First Aid Box to draw from when we need them. I want you to go away from this book with a whole host of strategies that you can incorporate seamlessly into your life, regularly or even if they are just now and then. However, fundamentally, if the stress is hitting and you feel you have nowhere to go, I want you to have your Emotional First Aid Box to draw from whenever you need it. Grab your favourite notebook and pen — if you don't have one you love, maybe it's time to treat yourself! I'm going to guide you through some questions to help you turn this book into a personal journey of self-discovery, exploring what sparks your stress and what helps to calm its waters. Remember, we're all different, and your experience is uniquely yours.

How Do I Record What Goes In My Box?

Do whatever feels right for you. Maybe try a few ideas and see what works:

- Find a box and add physical items that symbolise your acts of self-care or add slips of paper to your box or even a small jar, with a description of what makes you feel good.
- Make a list in your favourite notebook.

- Create a list on your phone or your computer.
- Draw a box and sketch items or cut pictures out of magazines that symbolise the things that you can do that make you feel good (example below)

As you choose your self-care items for your box, it's important to include a mix of trusted favourites alongside new things you'd like to try. Remember that each day is different, what you need today may not be what you'll need tomorrow, which is why it's essential to have a variety of options to draw from.

For example, today a trip to the gym or a walk may be the very thing that clears your mind and reduces your stress. However, tomorrow that may not work and 10 minutes of mindfulness may be exactly what you need instead.

When you access your emotional first aid box, stay open to all possibilities. What your mind and body need may not always align with what you *think* they need. As odd as it may sound, trust what you're instinctively drawn to. If you ask yourself, "What do I need right now?" your body will naturally respond (and here's a little secret: our bodies always know the answer, we just forget to listen). This gentle self-awareness can lead you to what you truly need, not what the thinking mind assumes you need.

Don't automatically assume that if your body wants to move, you need to hit the gym or go for a run. Perhaps a slower, more mindful practice like yoga is what your body and mind are asking for. By regularly asking, "What do my mind and body need in this moment?", you'll find the answer comes more naturally. Don't second-guess it, simply listen and support it in the best way you can. This is exactly why having a range of options in your self-care box is so important.

You get to choose what goes into your emotional first aid box, make it easily accessible because when everything feels like it is getting on top of you, you are not likely to be able to initially access your list in your mind. You may need a visual representation.

Let's examine how you can reduce stress and prevent burnout. Trust me, we rarely see the signs that burnout is on its way until it hits.

Your History

Before we begin this journey, I want you to know that how you manage your stress is influenced by many factors: your genes, physiology, biology, your experiences of how your parents handled their stress, your childhood, and everything in between that has got you to where you are today.

We are all different, and how we cope, and our levels of resilience, vary as a result of all the factors above. The first thing to say is, PLEASE DO NOT COMPARE yourself to someone else. Also, do not judge yourself or others. We all have a complex tapestry of life experiences that shape who we are, and although we cannot change the past, we can change how we go forward in the future. Understanding yourself and where your strengths and weaknesses lie will enable you to focus on the areas that are unique to you and provide you with the wisdom to decipher what you need and when you need it and the power to CHOOSE what to change and how to change it.

The Mind And Body

Manage Your Mind

Stress is often a state of mind, yet as a society, we've crafted a narrative that portrays EVERYTHING as stressful. We've reached a point where being busy and stressed has become synonymous with success. But why is that?

When you're juggling work, social life, family, parenting, and relationships, it's easy to feel like there simply aren't enough hours in the day.

Life can be super busy, but it's important to recognise that much of this "busyness" is a choice. When our mindset is anchored in the belief of "I am stressed," our bodies respond by releasing Cortisol, often called the "stress hormone," which is like a double-edged sword in our body's toolkit. On the good side, it's the helper that kicks in when we need to rise to a challenge whether that's tackling a work deadline or keeping our cool when our kids are testing every ounce of patience. It helps regulate our blood sugar, reduces inflammation, and assists in memory formulation. But here's where it gets tricky: when we're in a constant state of stress… hello, modern parenting! Cortisol can turn into a bit of a bully. It starts to wear down our bodies, disrupts sleep, lowers immunity, and can leave us feeling frazzled and exhausted. Like most things in life, it's about balance, using that surge of cortisol when we need it but not letting it run the show.

Shifting our mindset can help to mitigate the amount of cortisol triggers we experience. Changing our thinking from "I am stressed" to "I am busy" sends a different message to the brain, leading to a more measured physiological response less cortisol and more balance. The way we think and the words we choose can profoundly shape how we feel.

"Where focus goes, energy flows."

Remember when you first found out you were having a baby! Suddenly, pregnant women seemed to be everywhere, right? Subconsciously, you were seeking out your tribe. The same thing happens when you buy a new car, you start seeing that same make and model all around you. The brain, while complex, operates on simple principles. The saying "Where focus goes, energy flows" is particularly relevant to our thoughts. We naturally zoom in on what's important to us at any given moment, making it appear more prominent in our world.

If we're stressed and anxious, we tend to focus on everything that's going wrong, reinforcing the belief that "today is going to be a bad day" and amplifying our stress and anxiety. Conversely, when we're happy and content, the brain highlights those positive aspects, making us more likely to overlook minor hiccups like forgetting to buy more milk. In both cases, our feelings intensify as our focus sharpens.

Now, let's consider how this plays out in our daily lives. Imagine you wake up in the morning after a pretty terrible nights sleep, and before you've even had a chance to get out of bed or savour your first cup of coffee, everything seems to be falling apart. The baby is screaming, you realise you forgot to take the washing out of the machine last night, and to top it all off somebody has drank the last of the milk. All this before you've even considered the rest of the day's demands. Sound familiar?

It's easy to get swept up in the "this is a nightmare" mindset, setting the stage for a stressful day.

But what if we break down these moments individually rather than letting them compound into one overwhelming experience?

- **The baby is crying**. That's normal, crying is how babies communicate their needs. It doesn't mean they're unhappy, just that they need something. (But you already know this, right?)
- **You forgot to hang up the washing last night.** It happens. You're human, and humans occasionally drop the ball. That's perfectly okay.
- **You've run out of milk**. Who made you the milk police? Did you know it was running low, or did someone else forget to mention it?

Or did you simply forget to nip to the shop yesterday? Either way, it's not the end of the world. Maybe it's a black coffee and toast kind of morning, and that's totally fine.

In isolation, each of these morning challenges is something you've handled before. However, when juggling multiple tasks simultaneously, the stress response intensifies, and before we know it, we're metaphorically tearing our hair out.

As adults, we often create countless unspoken rules that we equate with success whether it's always having milk in the fridge, making sure everyone is where they need to be on time, or keeping the cupboard stocked "just in case" someone might want something. These seemingly small rules can quietly add to our stress because when we don't meet them, a part of us feels like we've failed.

The sooner we recognise that we're meant to be imperfect, that we're fallible and not designed to get everything right all the time, the easier it becomes to give ourselves permission to let go. It's okay if things don't go perfectly. Instead of feeling like a failure, we can simply say, "Oops; never mind it's not the end of the world. Maybe I just need to adjust the shopping list to buy more milk."

How we interpret situations, especially when they're layered on top of each other, can significantly increase our stress levels. But if we take a moment to break them down and view them individually, suddenly, the day shifts from "this is a nightmare" to "this is normal life." The baby will eventually stop crying, the washing will get hung up or rewashed, and tomorrow, there will be milk. Adopting a more positive outlook can even change the course of the day because, let's be honest, we've all had moments where we think, "It's going to be one of those days," and then it becomes exactly that, simply because our mindset is focused on the challenges rather than the successes.

Next time your day starts in a 'bad' way, just try telling yourself "This is just a moment in time, and despite how the day has begun, today is going to be a good day" and see what happens.

FLIP THE SCRIPT

Life is full of daily challenges, but what if we

flipped the word 'challenge' to 'opportunity'? Every experience offers a chance to grow and thrive, but that all depends on our internal dialogue. If we view something as stressful, it will feel stressful. If we see it as an opportunity, we're more likely to embrace it, grow, and enjoy the journey. Ultimately, we often overcome what we face, so why not approach it positively?

Your mind can be your best friend or your worst enemy!

We often speak to ourselves in ways we'd never dream of talking to someone else. It's important to be kind to yourself. You have the potential to be your own best friend but to do so, you need to find the space to be compassionate towards yourself. Remember, you're not perfect, nobody is. In fact, perfection doesn't actually exist, so be kind.

PERFECTIONISM

If you're a perfectionist, this will likely resonate with you. As parents, it's natural to want to be the best we can be and to model excellence for our children by striving to excel in all areas of life. But this can be utterly exhausting, especially when perfection is an illusion. Yet so many of us chase it.

Think about it: we set ourselves tasks to complete 'perfectly', but when we achieve them, we rarely take time to celebrate. Instead, we often find flaws in our successes and immediately consider how to improve. This is why perfection is unattainable, we keep moving the goalposts. As a result, we never truly experience the sense of achievement we're seeking, and we continue striving for more. Worse still, this often leads to a persistent feeling of inadequacy because the thing we set out to do perfectly was not perfect after all and therefore, the sense of failure kicks in. There is no value in chasing perfection. Removing the concept of 'perfect' from not only your mind but also your family home is a great step towards ensuring your children don't strive for the impossible.

That's not to say that we shouldn't strive to grow and achieve in whatever way we choose. However, perfectionist tendencies can undermine our self-esteem and confidence.

A question to consider:

Am I a perfectionist?

If so, *Where did that come from?*

Who in my life also strives for perfection?

It's possible you may have inherited this trait from one of your parents, or perhaps you push yourself to achieve more than others to feel confident and worthy because maybe you feel you have something to prove.

Now ask yourself:

How has this served me in my life?

Do you feel satisfied with your drive to achieve, or has this trait more often left you feeling exhausted, constantly needing to do better, and never feeling 'good enough'?

Perfectionism is rarely helpful. It pushes us to chase something that doesn't exist, often leaving us with a lingering sense of failure. It is so easy to see how people who are perfectionists or who are constantly striving for the next thing often suffer from stress.

If this is you, then; let's look at changing the

narrative and start with:

"Doing my best is good enough".

Now this may feel a little clunky because when you first start changing how you speak to yourself, it may feel awkward, inauthentic, or even untrue. But let's think of your brain as a network of roads. Every new thought and idea creates a new neural pathway or road, which, if used frequently, becomes more robust. On the flip side if the thought is not repeated, then the neural pathway withers away.

You could also think of this as a muscle, the more we use a muscle the stronger it becomes. The less we use a muscle the weaker it becomes. Our neural pathways work the same way. If you constantly tell yourself, "I'm not good enough," that pathway becomes a deep groove in your brain—a well-travelled road that feels like the truth. But if you start to repeat, "I am good enough," over and over, you're paving a new road. And with practice, this road becomes the one your brain naturally takes. The more you repeat this new narrative, the more your brain embraces it, turning it into your new reality.

It's crucial to teach our children, by example, that doing our best is good enough and that perfection is unattainable. Dropping the ball occasionally shows our children that we can pick it up again. What we do in life doesn't define us, who we are, our values and our morals are what truly define us. Life is full of challenges; as humans, we're not designed to succeed at everything. We are fallible; we make mistakes and get things wrong, but we can learn from our experiences and strive to be the best version of ourselves. Let's be clear though, this isn't about being perfect because perfection simply doesn't exist.

"I thrive on stress."

Really? Or do you thrive on the sense of accomplishment that lights you up? There is such a thing as 'eustress', often referred to as 'positive stress', which is likely where the phrase "I thrive on stress" originates. There's nothing wrong with wanting to succeed and thrive; however, there's a risk of becoming somewhat addicted to the feel-good sensation associated with potential success. This can lead to a pattern of constantly seeking out big challenges and opportunities so as to trigger the brain's reward system and release the "feel good" hormone Dopamine.

I have seen more and more over the years how people consciously and subconsciously trigger a dopamine kick, I would even go as far as to say that dopamine can be a little addictive. We all experience a dopamine release when we are looking forward to something, like when we tick a job off our list (I've been known to add things just to tick them off!), the anticipation of that glass of wine at the end of the day or the bar of chocolate waiting in the fridge. We all love that feel-good sensation, and once we learn how to trigger it, our brains naturally seek it out. But like everything it's all about balance and our bodies are built to handle short bursts of stress, but too much, even of the good kind needs managing, just like wine and chocolate.

Think about how often you feel stressed, whether it's days in a week, weeks in a month, or even most of the year all in the name of chasing that one or even many goals. And when you finally achieve them, how long do you actually savour that moment of accomplishment before diving headfirst into the next task or project? Consider how many other parts of your life might be taking a backseat due to this relentless drive and focus in one area of your life. To top it off the chances are the stress and pressure far outweigh the fleeting moments of satisfaction. So, the real question is, can you achieve the same success without all the stress (remember we are essentially talking about internal chatter that fires up the cortisol release)? What is it about the stress that makes you believe it's pushing you toward more effective results?

Chronic stress can take a toll on both mind and body and managing it is key to maintaining overall well-being.

Let's explore what can happen when stress overstays its welcome.

OUR BODIES

Our bodies do not like being flooded with cortisol, the hormone released when we experience a stress response. Stress is very closely linked with anxiety, which releases adrenaline. Both of these are valuable assets when we are in life-threatening situations. Once upon a time, this would have been in the guise of a sabre-toothed tiger when our survival was genuinely at risk. However, in today's world, the threat of not impressing our boss or, worse still, losing our jobs can also create a stress response because our lives as we know them may change. This can also filter into our parenting because the busier we are, the less we can show up as our best selves in anything we do, and for most parents, all we want is to be the best we can be for our children. Yet often they can get the very worst of us after a busy day when we are exhausted and completely wrung out. Then the negative chatter begins once they are tucked up in bed: "I've shouted again," or "I should have helped them with their homework, but I had that email to send." "Tomorrow will be a better day." (Does this sound familiar?) Understandably, all these things contribute to increasing stress, and although our bodies can cope with short intervals of stress, if stress becomes a constant state of being, it can then begin to impact our physical health.

Signs of stress can include:

- Headaches

- Rapid heart rate
- Insomnia
- Rapid breathing
- Low sex drive
- Tense muscles
- Stomach ache
- Low mood
- Irritability
- Emotional exhaustion
- Using coping mechanisms to relax or self-soothe (Alcohol, Drugs, Gambling, Food)

As a result, this can impact our overall immune system, as well as our central nervous system, cardiovascular system, digestive system, and much more.

Stress is not worth it.

It brings nothing to the party and can deplete our mental, psychological, and physical well-being.

Before we look at key tips to reduce and manage stress, I want you to ask yourself a few questions to set the foundation for how you have reached this point in your life where stress is a part of it. Try not to overthink these questions; just go with the first thing that pops into your mind.

What am I gaining from being so busy?

For example, I feel valuable, I like achieving many things simultaneously, it distracts me from my thoughts, I receive praise from others, it's what others expect of me etc

Now, ask yourself why?

Why do I feel valuable? Why do I like achieving lots of things? Why do I want to be distracted from my thoughts? Why do I want to receive praise from others? Why do others expect this of me?

Being busy and stressed can serve us in many ways. It can be an attempt to feel good about ourselves or for others to give us positive feedback, OR keeping busy can distract us from how we think and feel about ourselves or our lives. Identifying how being stressed and busy serves us is the first step to finding balance in our lives. Humans do not do anything altruistically (solely for the purpose of another); we always have something to gain from everything that we do, even if it is causing us harm. Understanding the root of our reason why, enables us to address the foundation of what is driving the busyness and stress.

Consider the following

Does my sense of worth come from being all things to all people?

If yes, *ask yourself why.*

I.e. People might not like me, I may be rejected.

How do you feel about people who prioritise themselves mainly?

I.e. I think they are selfish or I so wish I could be more like that.

If our self-worth is steeped in other people's opinions, we are forever chasing that next bit of praise from others. The reality is that you cannot control what others think. You could be the most amazing person in the world, but somebody will always think otherwise. Being true to yourself and being the person that you want to be provides you with an automatic sense of high self-worth and self-esteem and any positive feedback that you receive becomes an added bonus. But because it is not expected or needed, you don't get that disappointing slump that comes when hoping for that praise and didn't receive it.

Compassion on the other hand provides us with the flexibility to be fallible humans but still be kind to ourselves.

Let me explain: As children, we are often taught vehemently to be compassionate towards others. Maybe with statements like "be kind to others", and "put others before yourself", how often does somebody bump into us and WE say sorry… what is that about? Anyway, I digress… my point is that when are we encouraged to have the same compassion for ourselves? Often we are not and this needs to change. Compassion is not indulgence or having an inflated view of yourself, it is simply a mindset that we can access that accepts our fallibility, it's a place where we don't make excuses for our downfalls but we learn from them. We also do not beat ourselves up for making a mistake we approach it from a compassionate place and rather than say something like "OMG I am so stupid, what an idiot" we may say something like "I made a mistake there and I feel pretty bad, but that's ok because feeling sad and low or angry or scared is normal when we make a mistake. What can I learn from this and how can I rectify it"

Going back to the concept that we can be our best friend or our worst enemy, compassion is the linchpin for this because all the time we can be kind to ourselves even when we are feeling at our most challenged we can overcome anything. Being unkind to ourselves elevates our stress and fear responses within our bodies which leads us to a place of burnout. BE KIND you have nothing to lose and everything to gain.

On the point of how you feel about others if they prioritise themselves mainly; if you believe them to be a little selfish or self-focused, a question to ask yourself is, are they stressed in their life? Are they as busy? Or have they got an enviable balance? There is a good chance that you may think the latter.

But here are a few questions to ponder.

Do I fear failure?

If yes, *ask yourself why.*

I.e., I will feel useless, I will let people down, I will be criticised, etc.

EVERYBODY fails at times. With failure

comes growth. Nobody likes feeling like they have failed, but this is all part of human life. If you see your failings as room for growth, you win. We rarely grow from our successes, as we often don't reflect on them and see if there is room for growth because we succeeded. Whereas our failings, OMG, we tend to reflect on them a TON. See this as a positive process. You have so much to gain from what you don't succeed in, and then when you do hit the jackpot, it will be all the sweeter.

Do I struggle to say no?

If yes, *ask yourself why.*

I.e. I don't want to disappoint people or make them think I can't cope.

What do you think of people who say no?

I.e., they are lazy, they don't consider others They are selfish.

People who can balance Yes and NO often have positive mental health. They think carefully about their decision and whether they can fulfil that commitment. Learning about our personal limits is so important. The more we say yes to people, the more likely they will come to us first with a request. The reality is that if we were to say no, that person would still find somebody to do what they have asked for; they would just explore other avenues.

This is where employers really struggle because if they have a member of staff who always says yes, they may have little idea that person is feeling overloaded. Until, of course, the yes person becomes burnt out and needs time off to recover. No employer wants this, and we as individuals must put the boundaries in place and learn the art of NO.

Our lives are not lived in boxes and our ability to cope is based on multiple factors, all of which fluctuate all of the time.

For example, a 45-year-old person with few home life pressures and commitments is likely to experience more energy and focus than a 45-year-old who has teenagers, and young children together with ailing parents. FACT. That doesn't mean both are not equally good at their jobs, however the latter, without a doubt will have a sense of being pulled in many directions and may feel stress, anxiety and frustration more keenly as a result of the compound nature of the pressure they are under. Therefore, learning to say no is crucial especially when life hits and the pressure is on. Many employers, family members and friends would far prefer we learn the art of NO rather than becoming unwell as a result of trying to be all things to all people. NO definitely needs to become part of all of our vocabulary and within our ability to set our boundaries.

If you resonate with the above questions and can see that potentially your sense of self-worth is steeped in busyness and potentially stress, then I would like you to ask yourself the following:

Who taught you that being busy and/or stressed was a good thing?

This may be a simple message that you were told, like 'You must work hard', or did you watch one of your parents prioritise others or work long hours and learn that this is all part of adulting?

This is where we start to explore generational patterns. Our parents and their parents were raised in very different eras, and society's expectations differed. The role of being a parent has changed significantly even in the last couple of decades as we learn more about children's emotional needs. The family's wants and needs have also changed. Many children have extracurricular activities that they need funding and ferrying to. Of course, we have experienced the birth of technology and the internet, which has, in many ways, made things more efficient but has also increased our expectations of ourselves and others. More women work than ever; therefore, men's roles have also changed. Yet we carry our parents' and grandparents' subliminal life and parenting messages, almost ignoring the societal changes and simply expecting ourselves to shoulder the extra seemingly invisible workload. We have to stop and re-evaluate and manage our expectations of ourselves. Some of you reading this may not want your children to feel as you do right now, but in fact, they are watching you and learning all about what an adult does, how they navigate their lives, manage their emotions, and the stress in their lives. One last question at this point:

Would you want your future adult child to feel as you do right now?

If the answer is no, *why is it ok for you to feel as you do now?*

Let's explore key stress management tips and why they will make a difference. I know you already know the standard tips, like exercising more and eating better because I'm guessing you've googled the hell out of this subject, but let's look at not just the 'what' to do but also the 'how' and the 'why'.

THE EMOTIONAL FUEL TANK

If you remember what I said at the beginning, burnout doesn't just hit, it silently creeps up and we tend to ignore the warning signs because until it hits we don't realise they are warning signs.

The Emotional fuel tank is a concept I use when working with all of my clients. When we are fresh out of emotional energy not only can we burn out but this is also when our mental health can take a nose dive. I want you to be able to take control of this before you become emotionally exhausted as it is far harder and takes longer to recover if we allow our emotional energy to run too low.

I remember when I was seventeen my dad told me not to run my fuel tank in my car down too low as we, at the time, had leaded fuel and if run too low he said it would pull up the sludge from the bottom of the tank and it will make the engine sluggish and affect the performance of the car. Which is what I liken our emotional energy to. If we run too low then our emotional, psychological and physical wellbeing becomes sluggish. So let's take a look at what this fuel tank business is all about.

Imagine you have two fuel tanks. One that stores your physical energy and the other that stores your emotional energy.

Our physical fuel tank requires food, drink, and sleep to remain topped up and if we start depleting in those areas our bodies respond. So if we start to feel hungry we need food, if we need water we start to feel thirsty and if we are tired we need to sleep. Therefore we are pretty good at keeping ourselves alive by responding to our physical needs.

Our emotional energy is the same, but the messages are far more subtle, and this is why we sometimes miss the signs.

Like our physical energy, our emotional energy is depleting and fluctuating all of the time. So let's imagine a tap at the bottom of our emotional fuel tank that you can't quite turn off and all day every day our emotional energy is depleting. Every person we come into contact with, every thought we have, everything we do impacts our emotional energy. But the question is how do we know what is depleting our emotional energy and what is fueling it?

DEPLETION

Human beings tend to take our energy. When we interact with other people we are conscious of what we are saying, and how we are behaving and we are impacted by the things they are doing too. So if our friend is struggling in their marriage the chances are they are offloading in an attempt to feel better. As a result, our emotional energy is depleting. Which is fine, if we are managing to refuel sufficiently. Our friends, family, work, our thoughts about finances health, and anything and everything we care about or that bothers us in some way are depleting our emotional energy. Then when we least expect it something BIG can happen, like redundancy, or a bereavement and our tap opens up and starts dumping all the emotional energy we have because we are trying to come to terms with the curve ball life has just thrown us. It's easy to see how before we know it we are emotionally exhausted if this is left unchecked.

On a day-to-day basis, we rely on human beings who are taking our emotional energy to refuel us equally. However, we know that if our friend is struggling in her marriage the chances are she doesn't have the headspace or emotional energy herself to support whatever is going on in our world. So we have less emotional energy as a result.

Imagine if, over months and years, you are using more emotional energy than you are refuelling with, it's not difficult to see that eventually, you may start to run low, but we generally only recognise this when we become sluggish. A telltale sign that we are emotionally exhausted is when we get a good night's sleep yet wake up feeling as exhausted as the day before. If you are finding this is happening then it would be a good idea to have a chat with your Doctor to rule out any medical concerns however in the absence of it being anything medical I would encourage you to take a good look at what and who is depleting you and what and who is refuelling you.

Consider the following:

- Is there anybody in my life that takes more of my emotional energy than they give?
- Is there anybody in my life who takes as much as they give?
- Is there anybody in my life that I take more of their emotional energy than I give?
- Do my thoughts mainly refuel me or deplete me?

These are all great questions to ask yourself to identify areas of depletion and also highlight shifts that may need to take place in your relationships. This is not to say that you should change your relationships but for example, if you are feeling emotionally depleted then give the person in question A) a wide berth until you are energised.

So what is the answer?

FREE Energy

Free energy fuelers are things in your life that take NOTHING. Usually, they don't include other human beings, because remember that when interacting with others this automatically takes, or if these things do include humans you may find that although it takes a little from it adds soooo much more. Some examples

- Exercise
- Meditation/mindfulness/grounding techniques
- Interests/hobbies – the list of these is endless
- Nature

Anything that provides you with a space to switch your mind off to the noise of the world and requires you to focus on this one thing essentially gives your active mind a rest.

Although we know that too much screen time and gaming is not good for a child's developing mind. What we have to acknowledge is that often children immerse themselves in these activities and as a result, they enter into a world a little bit like I may have done when I was a child when reading the latest Enid Blyton book and as a result has a similar effect. So although too much screen time should be avoided, downtime should be encouraged and for all of us, our version of downtime and emotional refuelling differs.

It would be a great idea to encourage each member of your family to explore where they get their free emotional energy from. This will help both you and them to identify what they need and when they need it, which will help to foster a calmer more harmonious household.

Emotions Scale

So now we know a little more about our emotional energy and how it ebbs and flows, lets start collecting some data so that you can begin to notice when your tap is opening up and draining and when it is closing and refuelling. Create a scale of 0 (not at all) to 10 (extreme) in your mind's eye when thinking about how you feel. As we are talking about stress, let's try that out.

So, without analysing or overthinking it, on a scale of 0-10, how stressed are you right now? You may have had an immediate number pop into your mind. If you didn't, don't worry; just take the first number you think of. The more you do this exercise, the more your body will show you a number that is true to how you feel right now (Woo Woo again, but trust me when I say before you know it you will hear/feel a number).

You can use this scale to identify the intensity of anything you are feeling, and with this awareness, you can learn more about what you need to help manage that emotion. If you are above a five, something must change RIGHT NOW. Don't let it get to an eight or a nine, because by then you are pulling your hair out and ready to escape to an uninhabited island somewhere in Scotland, and I'm not sure your kids would like that.

Our emotions are at the epicentre of everything we do, not least how we cope with stress. Let's look at ways to bring any emotions which are peaking above a 5 down. Not all of these tips will be for you but pick the ones that you lean towards and maybe flirt with the ones that feel a little uncomfortable as you never know, that strategy may become your new best friend if you embrace it.

Self-Care

1) Take A Breath

This tip will be repeated throughout this book because taking a breath can change everything within a literal heartbeat. As adults, we tend to breathe shallowly, with our chest moving up and down. If you watch a baby or young child breathing while sleeping, you will see them breathing into their tummies. Our bodies need oxygen to survive; however, as adults, we often take in the bare minimum to sustain life. If we breathe into our tummies, we inject more oxygen into our bloodstream, organs, and, not least, our brain, and it calms our central nervous system, which is the motherboard of our alert and rest-and-digest system. If you want to test this, put a hand on your chest and a hand on your tummy.

See which one rises when you are breathing naturally. Breathing can create a reset for our minds and calm our nervous system when we are anxious or stressed.

Let's give it a go: Imagine you have a balloon in your tummy, and your job is to blow it up, not so much that it's about to pop, but enough to look like a balloon.

Breathe in through your nose for the count of 3, following your breath down through your chest, through your diaphragm (which is the muscle at the bottom of your rib cage), and into your tummy. Then, breathe out for the count of 3 through your mouth. You can extend this to the count of 4, but if you really want to give your body a treat, then breathe in for the count of 3 through your nose and out for the count of 6 through your mouth. Again, you can extend this by breathing in for 4 (through your nose) and out for 8 (through your mouth).

Now go back to your scale of 0-10 and ask yourself, 'How stressed am I now?' There is a good chance the numbers have dropped. See, it works.

2) Slow Everything Down.

I appreciate that this is easier said than done. However, if your life is frenetic and you feel like you are constantly chasing your tail, something needs to give, and this doesn't have to be at your cost. Adjust your commitments based on where you are today.

3) Prioritise Sleep

Establish a regular sleep routine to ensure adequate rest. If you have a child who doesn't sleep or a young baby, expecting a straight eight hours of sleep is likely unrealistic, but try to rest where possible. Sleep doesn't start when you hit the pillow. The things you do leading up to going to bed are also factors.

- Reduce or eliminate caffeine from your diet. Caffeine increases adrenaline levels, which exacerbate stress and anxiety.
- Eat your last meal as early as possible. Digestion disrupts sleep quality, and even evening snacking can contribute to disrupted sleep.
- Spray a lavender scent on your pillow.

- Have a warm bath.
- Reduce screen time directly before bed.
- Quiet your mind by listening to a soothing meditation before settling into sleep.
- Reduce or eliminate alcohol, as this can significantly reduce the quality of sleep.
- Pop a notepad next to your bed so that if you do happen to wake in the night with racing thoughts then you have a way of emptying them from your mind until you wake in the morning.

I think we have all experienced nocturnal worry and find ourselves thinking 'Oooh I mustn't forget that' at 3 am (eeek). It is exactly this that keeps our brain awake as it is actively working on remembering the information, not to mention all the things we worry about that strangely do not appear to be a worry at 8 am (aarrghh) . Think about it this way: when we go to sleep our conscious (awake) mind goes off-line, however, whilst we are sleeping our subconscious mind is still happily awake and because it doesn't have the conscious mind to keep it in check, then the mind is its very own playground. When we are stressed and anxious in our awake state this can then continue whilst we are asleep which is why our anxiety feels far worse when it erupts in the night. This is simply because the conscious mind hasn't been able to play a part in being able to rationalise the ruminating and catastrophising thoughts.

As parents, we cannot mitigate the disruptions our children cause us at night, but the quality of sleep far outweighs the quantity, so if you can get a few hours of good sleep by making a few small changes, you are more likely to be refreshed for the day ahead.

4) Exercise Regularly

Incorporate physical activity into your daily routine to boost energy and mood. This doesn't mean a 5-mile run or two hours in the gym. Take the time for a short walk in the fresh air. Even taking the dog for a walk can be a form of exercise rather than just seeing it as another job that needs doing (there's that mindset thing again). Exercise is great for the body, but its impact on our overall mental health is far greater. Ask yourself, why have you chosen to exercise before? Is it because you wanted to lose some weight? Or did you want to tone up? When you have been for that run or spent that time in the gym, did your body immediately reflect back at you with the results that you craved? NO. However, if you change your mindset about exercise and start to see it as fuel for your mind, you will win every time.

Let me give you an example: You feel tired, but you know you need to do your workout because if you are going to flatten that stomach or increase those abdominals, then you have to stick to your plan. You go into the gym flat and fatigued, yet you come out invigorated and accomplished. Yes, your body will have changed slightly, but this will not likely be visible to you now. This is why so many people give up on exercise; the results are not immediate. But what is immediate is the impact it has on our minds. Physiologically, exercise boosts endorphins, which are our natural antidepressants. It boosts mood, releases tension in the body, creates clarity in the mind, supports sleep, and strengthens our immune systems.

Exercise is also the antidote when our bodies are filled with adrenaline and cortisol as a result of anxiety and stress. When we become anxious, our bodies are flooded with adrenaline due to the brain's threat system triggering the fight, flight or freeze response. There it is right there… Our body goes into FIGHT or FLIGHT, yet often we sit at our desks and our brains bounce from one thing to another and become foggy. Our heart beats faster and breathing becomes shallow or erratic. There is less oxygen going to the brain to make it function optimally therefore we can't think straight and find ourselves fumbling to construct a sentence that makes sense.

When we enter the freeze response, it's as if our whole system shuts down. Our breathing becomes shallow, and we can feel completely zoned out or disconnected. In the animal kingdom, this response is a literal survival tactic when faced with a predator. Animals "play dead" (FREEZE) in the hopes that the predator will lose interest, thinking the "meat" isn't worth eating.

Triggering our threat system can feel extremely disempowering mentally and emotionally but can also leave us feeling wobbly physically.

The one thing our bodies naturally want and

need when we are anxious is for us to move. It has created all this adrenaline so that we can secure our survival by fighting, running or freezing and yet we are simply sitting.

Exercise is the perfect antidote to anxiety as we are physically working the adrenaline out. Spending 30 minutes exercising makes us significantly more mentally and emotionally productive in every area of our lives. It beats procrastinating and spending 30 minutes scrolling on social media or playing Candy Crush (maybe Candy Crush is just a me thing).

If you feel stressed or anxious, take a break and move. I promise you that you will feel better and more productive by taking that time.

5) Eat A Balanced Diet

Nourish your body with healthy foods to maintain physical and mental health. Again, you know this, but that doesn't change the fact that you may lean into that glass of wine or bar of chocolate to release some of that stress. Try to be mindful of why you are leaning towards them. Is it because you deserve it after a hard day? Is it because you want to feel some comfort, and wine or chocolate symbolises switching off? Is it because you've had a good day and you want to celebrate? This is all mindset stuff again. We anchor our beliefs to justify our actions, but does alcohol make you feel better? Does chocolate make you feel better? Or after you've had the wine or chocolate, is there a tinge of regret, "Argh, that gym session was a waste of time now," or "I don't feel great this morning as I had one glass too many"? Although alcohol does indeed shut down the threat system temporarily, giving us that lovely feeling that the mind is quieter and we feel like we can rest, this is often only the case when we are consuming it. Sadly, it not only disrupts our quality of sleep, but it wakes us up approximately four hours after we've consumed our last drink, and the threat system goes into overdrive, which leaves us more anxious and often low in mood, not to mention feeling tired and a little jaded in readiness for yet another busy day. This cycle is common for many people. I would recommend trying three months of abstinence from alcohol, but if that feels too much, then start drinking with awareness. Just notice when you reach for that glass of wine or the chocolate. Very often we lean towards our coping mechanisms without awareness and consume far more than we would actually like. Choose to drink or eat chocolate and give yourself permission with awareness. When you do this, you are more likely to let go of the negative chatter that comes after it because you made a conscious choice rather than being driven by habit and the subconscious beliefs that drive such actions.

If you are stressed or anxious and lean towards a food type or alcohol to self-soothe, start by asking yourself the following questions:

Why do I want this?

Am I trying to make myself feel better? (If so, could you do something different such as distract yourself at wine o'clock or when you would normally have the chocolate? You would be amazed how effective this can be.)

Is this a habit I have created? (How long have you been doing this thing?)

How did I learn that this is a habit to have? (Did your parents use the same things to self-soothe?)

Would I be happy for my child to self-soothe in this way? (Remember that children are watching how we cope in life and are likely to repeat the cycle.)

Another area to consider is caffeine. Try to eliminate caffeine from your daily lifestyle. Caffeine stimulates adrenaline release, so if you are already stressed or anxious, this is likely to exacerbate that. This does not mean you can never have coffee again, but monitor how you are feeling and whether your system is emotionally fuelled sufficiently to take the caffeine hit. Remember caffeine increases adrenaline, which drains your emotional energy, so check in on how much emotional fuel you have and whether coffee is a wise idea today.

6) Take Breaks

Schedule short breaks throughout the day to recharge. Now that more and more people are working from home, it is easy to sit at your desk and stay there without interruption for an entire day. Schedule short breaks. Equally, if you are at home with the kids, make sure you sit down with that cup of tea and take a breather. Nothing requires 24/7 running around; this mental break will refuel your emotional energy.

7) Practice Mindfulness

Engage in mindfulness or meditation exercises to stay grounded. Mindfulness is simply a mind shift to being completely in the present. It can be really tough initially, but a great way to start mindfulness is when you brush your teeth for two minutes. Put all of your focus on brushing your teeth, how the brush feels in your mouth, and the feel of the toothpaste. Notice each of the strokes whilst brushing. Another quick mindfulness technique you can use is to feel your feet on the floor and your butt on your chair. Notice where your hands are resting and the texture of what is underneath them. This gives your brain a short rest, and you are fully in the present. We spend so much time in the past and in the future (which often breeds stress and anxiety) that we often miss the present. There are lots of free 5-10 minute meditations that are accessible online to plug yourself into and give your brain a rest.

Something I love doing to reground myself is standing barefoot on the grass. This may feel too far out of your reach to consider, but grounding ourselves to the earth's core supports our energetic system, and standing on damp grass with bare feet can help us feel reconnected with ourselves. Scientific evidence suggests that such practices also help reduce electrical tensions in our bodies created by technology. So essentially it gives us a little detox. This is also why we benefit from walking through saltwater on the beach, as it is an incredible electrical conductor to the earth's core. Of course, when you are on holiday, you are likely to be more relaxed; however, walking or standing in a natural saltwater source can provide many physical, mental, and emotional benefits. In the absence of the beach, dewy grass is a great option, but even if you simply take your socks and shoes off and spend a few minutes barefoot on the grass, dewy or not, this can quickly reduce your sense of overwhelm and stress.

8) Seek Support

Don't hesitate to reach out to friends, family, or a support group. DO NOT be a martyr. Ask for help when you need it. This is not a sign of you failing. You are simply navigating life. Remember, not many years ago, children were born into communities where parents, grandparents, aunties, and uncles lived a few streets away. Now we grapple with the cost of childcare and use our childcare favours during the working week by getting grandparents involved. Consider outsourcing some of your jobs. Maybe invest in a cleaner. The hours you save may be worth every penny for the cost of somebody else making your house nice and shiny in half the time.

9) Pursue Hobbies

Make time for activities you enjoy outside of parenting and life commitments. We all need a little bit of 'Me Time' even if that's escaping into a book. Hobbies outside of the home can often be tricky with little people, but find something just for YOU where possible. Whatever it is, ensure it is something you can access easily. With this comes a mutual conversation with your partner or your children's other parent. Make an agreement that you both get scheduled 'Me Time' and make sure you both stick to it, even if there needs to be a little flexibility at times. Having 'Me Time' can remind us that we are individuals in our own right outside of the many hats we all wear as a parent, a partner, a daughter/son, a sibling, or an employee, which can leave us with a sense of losing ourselves if we don't take the time to reconnect with ourselves.

10) Stay Hydrated

Drink plenty of water to keep your body functioning optimally (many sources recommend around 3 litres a day). Stress can cause dehydration, and dehydration can contribute to stress. You can easily do this very simple thing to support your body's system. Stress can result from multiple factors, so staying hydrated can mitigate the build-up.

11) Set Boundaries

Learn to say no and set limits to avoid overcommitment. How many times have you found yourself saying yes when you actually mean no? This is a common issue for many people, and as I said earlier in this book, we have to take a breath and consider our answer before responding. If you are unsure, say 'Can I get back to you?'. If saying no means that somebody doesn't like you, or in some way, this affects your relationship with them, then you have to consider whether they were really your kind of person. When we care for somebody, we respect their boundaries, so implementing boundaries is essential in every relationship, not least as a parent. Again, your child is watching the boundaries you set and will likely follow your lead later in life. So, if you are a yes person and struggle to say no, you will find it difficult to teach your child healthy boundaries. Boundaries reduce the chances of us triggering a stress response because we are less likely to over-commit ourselves.

Emotional Well-Being

How we manage our emotions is at the centre of how we cope with life. Our emotional management has often been shaped in childhood based on how our parents taught us about emotion regulation. If one of your parents was explosive, there is a good chance either you or your partner can be explosive. If one of your parents was passive, then either you or your partner would likely be passive. How our parents may have coped with stress can be mirrored in us. This is as a result of modelling. Our parents teach us about emotions, beliefs, values, and behaviours. So let's look at how you can support your emotional management.

12) GET CLEAR ON WHAT YOU ARE FEELING

We have FOUR CORE emotions:
- Anger
- Sadness
- Happiness
- Fear

You may be able to see that stress is part of the FEAR family. So, let's focus on fear here, but you can ask yourself the same questions about the other three emotions.

How do you feel physically (in your body) when you are stressed/fearful?

I.e., knotty stomach, tense muscles, headache.

How do you behave when you are stressed or fearful?

I.e., Do you go quiet, shout, cry, or snap?

What triggers your stress/fear?

I.e., if I have too much on, if somebody speaks to me in a certain way, or if I feel like I've failed in some way.

Developing an awareness of your triggers can go a long way to helping you manage them and provide you with an opportunity to reframe them. An example of this might be:

"I am so stressed" vs "I am busy—what can I do to reduce my load?"

"I can't believe how that person spoke to me—how dare they?" vs. "I need to address that comment with that person. Maybe they are having a tough day, and they, too are stressed. It's not personal."

"I'm such a failure" vs. "This is a learning opportunity."

13) The Chaos Of Invalidation vs. The Power Of Validation

Picture the scene: You've had a bad day at work and come home to your partner, feeling really irritated with your boss.

You: I'm so angry. I've had such a bad day. My boss is unreasonable and just expects too much of me.

Your Partner: I don't know why you are angry; don't take it out on me, if you're unhappy, just leave.

You: I'm not taking it out on you and I don't want to leave; I'm just frustrated.

Your Partner: Well, I think you're being overly dramatic.

I don't doubt that you can resonate with this response. But I want you to ask yourself how it feels when this happens! You may feel even MORE irritated because you are now frustrated with both your partner and your boss. This is the chaos of invalidation. When we invalidate another person's feelings, we just exacerbate them, and the frustration becomes multilayered. This can hugely contribute to stress if we feel unsupported by the people closest to us even if their intention is quite the opposite.

This also applies to children. They come to us with what, seemingly to an adult, is an overemotional reaction to a fairly insignificant problem. Because as adults we judge the problem as insignificant, we can easily invalidate a child's feelings as a result. However, in their little world, that's the biggest thing going on for them right now in the same way that your frustration about your boss is the biggest thing for you right now. When we invalidate another's feelings, we are essentially judging them, and as a result, they become more emotional.

Validation is essential when anybody is feeling a particular emotion.

Picture the scene: You've had a bad day at work and come home to your partner, feeling really irritated with your boss.

You: I'm so angry. I've had such a bad day. My boss is unreasonable and just expects too much of me.

Your Partner: Let's sit down and you can tell me what's happened.

You: He's just really annoying and has piled another project on my already busy workload.

Your Partner: That sounds really tough, and I'm not surprised you are angry with him. Is there any way I can help you find a solution?

You: No, I just needed to talk about it. I will get it sorted; it's just been a challenging day, that's all.

Your Partner: I can see that, and it's okay to be angry. Would you like a cuddle?

How would you feel receiving this response?

Validation immediately reduces the power of the emotion. I'm not suggesting that it will disperse fully, but if you or somebody else is able to provide you with the compassion you need at this tricky time, it will help you manage the emotion more effectively.

In the absence of somebody else providing you with validation, try the following:

If you are feeling stressed, take a moment to say to yourself,

"It's understandable that I am feeling stressed right now as I have X, Y, and Z to do, and I don't actually know how I'm going to get it done, but I know I will."

Relationships and connection with others are key factors in our lives, and tension within our homes can cause us even more stress. Validation is your superpower when looking to help your own or somebody else's emotions disperse and is also an essential ingredient for thriving relationships.

Even if you do not know why your child is kicking off, or your partner is grumpy, validating how they feel will help their emotions disperse, opening up space for communication. We all need to feel that we have a soft place to land, whatever the world throws at us. Being kind and supporting other each other's emotions can go a long way to reducing stress, and anxiety and refuelling that emotional energy.

14) Separate Your Emotions From Others

Your emotions belong to you; their emotions belong to them. Whoever you are engaging with, whether it be your child, your partner, or your boss, remember they will be experiencing their emotions for reasons that are likely beyond your control. It is important to have boundaries in place so that you are treated respectfully, but separating your emotions from others is so important as this allows us to control the controllable. We can only control ourselves; we have no control over other humans, not even our children.

When somebody else is upset directly with us, it's not uncommon to try to defend ourselves because our emotions are triggered by their accusation. In this situation, the first port of call is to remind ourselves that their emotion is theirs and yours is yours. Let's go back to the scenario where the lady came home having had a bad day at work. She wasn't angry with her partner, yet her partner took Umbridge with how she was expressing her day and, therefore got defensive and dismissive.

In the revised scenario, he was able to completely de-personalise the situation and support her in the way that she needed.

We have to try and separate our emotions from others if we want to resolve situations with ease and prevent escalation. We are all entitled to differing opinions but little positive ground is covered when we are in conflict with another. Validation provides a platform to defuse situations and create an opportunity to communicate calmly.

15) LISTEN AND COMMUNICATE OPENLY

"A problem shared is a problem halved." This is a common saying and provides people with a sense of catharsis when expressing their emotions. As a result, it helps them process their thoughts and emotions and soon they disperse. I genuinely believe that as a society we have forgotten how to listen to each other, which is one of the reasons why therapists are in such demand. Sadly, our lives are so busy we often only half listen to people and as a result, this can create relationship challenges or can leave people including children feeling invisible.

Communicating in a healthy, calm, respectful way can prevent stress from developing and create opportunities for resolutions to be found. Responding to situations rather than reacting can make a huge difference in how we communicate (this is also where listening can play a huge part as we need to be clear on what has been said rather than half listening). A reaction is when we say things without thinking and a response is when we consider a response. A reaction is often driven by emotions and a response is more logical and measured.

I would encourage you to notice how often you give your undivided attention to somebody when they are speaking. Ensuring you are not thinking about anything other than what they are saying. This is really important when listening to our children especially if they are talking about their emotions as this helps them to develop their own emotional literacy and learn how to get their needs met healthily. If we are not listening to children with intention this is when they may become distressed in an attempt to get the attention they need. Remember, children will not likely always be able to articulate how they feel when they are young, but the more we encourage children to develop their emotional literacy and understanding, the more equipped they will be for the future. Also, it then gives you more of an opportunity to support them.

16) DON'T JUDGE YOUR EMOTIONS OR OTHERS'

Everybody feels something for a reason. No emotion is stupid, extreme, bad, overly sensitive, or excessive. Every emotion deserves acknowledgment even when we don't understand it. Acceptance of ourselves, and others, is key in this area. Only then can we begin to manage our emotions effectively.

17) MANAGE EXPECTATIONS

Accept that perfection is unattainable and focus on doing your best. This does not mean you will fall into a pit of laziness if you don't keep pushing yourself to unrealistic expectations; it simply means you can acknowledge your limitations and celebrate your achievements more frequently. This has a huge impact on confidence, self-esteem, and wellbeing. Be realistic. You are one human with 24 hours in a day. We often overestimate what we can do in a day and underestimate what we can do in a year.

This is also a great lesson for children. If you 'expect' yourself to tend to their every need immediately because you want to be the best parent you can be, then they will likely learn that this is how adults should be (not only that but it is exhausting). One of two things may happen. As they grow older, they may follow in your footsteps and expect themselves to meet the needs of others all of the time, ignoring their own needs (because essentially this is what you may have modelled). Conversely, they may not know how to prioritise others because they have always been the priority and therefore expect others to continue to meet their needs. Either way, this does not help relationships to thrive.

Being a parent is a fine balance, and supporting your child's growth by implementing age-appropriate independence is essential for their growth.

Managing the expectations of yourself and that of your child is important. As a result, your child is likely to have realistic expectations of themselves. This does not mean we shouldn't strive to achieve; it is about managing the expectations of ourselves so that we can mitigate unnecessary stress.

You are not perfect and that's okay.

18) WANT VS. NEED

First, just say in your mind's eye:

"I NEED to do the food shop."

How does that feel? Language is very powerful, and the term NEED sends a message to the brain that we are lacking something, and in order for our survival to be guaranteed, we NEED that thing. The brain doesn't care what the thing is; it just knows that you have specified it as a need, so it must be super important.

Now say the following: "I WANT to do the food shop."

When we use the word WANT, it sends a very different message to the brain: I can take it or leave it. We often get caught up in 'NEED'.

"I NEED to do X"

"I NEED to have Y"

NEED is about survival, and there is very little we NEED to survive: food, water, air, and connection (and a few more). But we don't NEED to do the shopping today (chances are there is plenty that you could cobble together for dinner). If you WANT to do the shopping today, that's great, but wanting doesn't fire up your survival system like NEED does. So, to reduce the compound effect of stress cortisol flooding your system, challenge the way in which you use the terms WANT and NEED.

19) LANGUAGE

How we use language and words can change how we feel in a heartbeat. If we go back to stress, very often we may just be busy, but we tell our brains that we are stressed, which can create a cortisol response.

- Develop an awareness of the words you use to describe situations or people or how you feel.
- Notice if there is a physiological or emotional response.

- Is there another way to verbalise your feelings that doesn't have such a profound impact?

It is common for humans to use extreme forms of language that can exacerbate what is already uncomfortable. For example, "I don't like that person" will create a slightly different response in the body than "I hate that person." Or maybe, "That person isn't very kind" vs. "That person is evil."

When we are managing our stress levels, this can be a delicate tapestry of multiple areas, some of which we are likely to have control over; language is one of them.

20) PRACTICE GRATITUDE

Reflect on the positive aspects of your life and parenting journey. Human beings tend to spend an inordinate amount of time focusing on the things that are wrong or ruminating on the fact that they are not where they want them to be. So they focus on the past and the future. At least once a day, think about the great things that have happened today. Did somebody smile at you in the street? Did the sun feel warm on your skin, or was the rain brilliantly watering your grass?

Having a little journal can be helpful as it allows you to jot down the great and sometimes really simple things that have happened today as a reminder that not every minute of every day is filled with stress.

21) Laugh Often

Find humour in daily life and enjoy moments of laughter with your children. You may recall that Happiness is one of our core emotions. However, sometimes we forget to smile and laugh because we are so caught up in the challenges of life. Laughter increases oxygen in the brain, so the body releases endorphins (much easier than all that exercise). Find opportunities to smile and laugh, even if you do not necessarily feel happy; it will signal a positive response in the brain and reduce stress and anxiety.

Smile at a stranger - It will not only brighten their day but yours too (even if they look confused, they can't miss that this complete stranger was smiling as they passed by).

Move away from the News - The news can create stress and anxiety because it is often steeped in negativity and things we have little control over.

Have you ever come across somebody who is ecstatic after they have watched a politician give their latest speech or learned more about the current war that has erupted within the world? The news can be an absolute joy thief.

Move towards comedy and light-hearted TV - Be mindful about what you watch on TV or social media if you are stressed. Police dramas, some sports (I actually don't understand why people watch football; I find it really stressful), horror movies–all of these can create an unnecessary stress response in the body, which is fine if we generally feel relaxed and rested, but when we are already stressed, programmes such as these can exacerbate it. Dive into a comedy or something that is relaxing and familiar.

Have you ever wondered why we watch a movie more than once? We all have at least one movie we have watched many times over the years; mine is Dirty Dancing. The reason is that we know what's coming. There are no surprises, and it's predictable. If we're feeling a little off-kilter, predictability provides us with comfort, so we lean into what we know.

Which is your Movie?

22) Seek Professional Help

Consult a therapist or counsellor if you feel stressed or overwhelmed. There is no shame in seeking external support. With the right therapist in place, you have the space to say things that you may never share with friends and family, and they will be received without judgment. This can hugely declutter the mind and provide you with the clarity and strategies you may need to overcome the challenges that you are facing. Here are a few tips if you want to seek professional support:

- Find the right person for you. Ask for a free initial chat with them. Generally, we get a feel for whether we like the sound of somebody within seconds or minutes of meeting or talking to them. Remember, this is your life, and you are precious cargo, so find somebody that you naturally warm towards. This will make the process much easier.
- More expensive doesn't necessarily mean a therapist is better.
- Take a look at their credentials and experience. A fancy qualification doesn't

always mean they are the right person for you, but it will give you some insight into the type of therapist they are and how much clinical experience they have had.

- If you are experiencing a particular difficulty that you want to resolve, then seek a specialist in that area.

- Research, research, research. You may not find the right therapist for you instantly, but isn't that the case with everything in life? We don't always meet our life partner as soon as we start dating. Sometimes we think that person may be right for us and then rethink it. Therapy can be the same. Some therapists may be able to take you so far, and then a change benefits your process. Although in an ideal world you will meet the right therapist for you the first time around, if you don't, then go back to the drawing board and find somebody that does suit you.

- Get recommendations from friends or family, although I will caveat this. The therapist who is right for your friend may not be right for you, so just bear that in mind. However, we often surround ourselves with like-minded people, so there is a good chance you too will benefit from the person recommended. But this is not definitive. Make your own decisions as to who is right for you.

- If you have been assigned a therapist through your employer and they are not suitable, ask to change. This is a perfectly acceptable request and should be honoured.
- If finances are an issue, speak to your GP about a referral to an NHS therapist. You may also find that multiple agencies within your area offer funded support or on a sliding scale.

23) Journal

Write down your thoughts and feelings to process emotions. Writing is the next best thing to speaking. It provides your brain with an outlet so that it's not whizzing with multiple thoughts and emotions simultaneously. This can be a really cathartic practice.

- You don't need to know what you want to write. Just write. Free writing is when we don't think about what we want to say. We just say it. You would be amazed at what comes out.

- If you are worried somebody else may read it, then destroy the page after you have written it. This process is for you and you only, unless you choose otherwise. Keep your thoughts and emotions safe.

- If you are angry with somebody or you are grieving the loss of somebody, write them an unsent letter. Write freely, maybe in a way that you would never speak to that person but get everything out onto paper (don't type it; handwritten is the way forward, as the physical act of writing is more powerful than typing). The brain is not concerned about whether you post the letter; it just recognises that it has been written; therefore, you will experience a lovely cathartic response. Then either keep it, tear it up into tiny pieces, or safely burn it. Do whatever you need to do to provide you with the release that you need. DO NOT SEND AN UNSENT LETTER. This can cause more stress than release.

24) CELEBRATE SMALL WINS

Acknowledge and celebrate small achievements and milestones. With the ongoing pressures in life, we tend to skip over the small wins. Celebrate them, even if it's just in your mind. It will help to refuel your emotional energy. For example:

- I did a great job there.
- I managed my child's tantrum really well there.
- Well done, me.

25) Practice Deep Breathing

Use deep breathing exercises to calm your mind. How many times have you heard this, that breathing can significantly reduce stress and anxiety and is literally the golden nugget we are all looking for? Yet we don't use it, because often we think "surely it can't be that easy, if it were nobody would be anxious'.

Well, it is and it isn't.

So, let's go back to the Fight, Flight or Freeze. This response is triggered by the Amygdala which is a small but mighty almond-shaped part of the brain. If you think about the amygdala as an alarm system that sounds when it identifies an actual or perceived threat. As a result, our vagus nerve jumps into action and adjusts the body so that we can respond to the threat at hand. For example, when anxious we often feel the need to empty our bowels, and this is so that the body is as light as possible for us to fight or flight (clever aye?). As a result, we are thrust into what is called our 'sympathetic system' which supports our need to muster up all of our energy to support our survival (remember when we are talking about survival our brain doesn't know that we are not going to be eaten by a sabre-toothed tiger all it knows is there is a threat).

Once the threat has passed our bodies need to settle back into 'rest and digest' which is the parasympathetic system. To move more quickly into this system we can utilise mindful breathing or the more clinical term Diaphragmatic breathing. This is like giving your vagus nerve a gentle hug, it's a simple, yet profoundly effective way to soothe your body's stress response. The vagus nerve is a key player in calming our nervous system. When we practice mindful breathing slowing down our inhales and extending our exhales we send a signal to the vagus nerve that says, "Hey, it's okay to relax now." This not only helps lower our heart rate and blood pressure but also shifts us out of that fight-or-flight mode and into a more grounded, centred state. It's like our very own inner reset button that helps us feel more present, balanced, and able to respond rather than react.

Now the reality is that rarely are we at physical threat from a sabre-toothed tiger, so this is where we can intervene early on when our threat system has been triggered and utilise mindful breathing to support our vagus nerve in moving back into the rest and digest system as early as possible.

For example:

You step off of the pavement right into the path of an oncoming bus.

Your inner alarm sounds and your amygdala goes to work sending adrenaline and signals to the body to prepare to fight or flight for survival.

You step back onto the pavement and the bus goes by.

However, your heart is still pumping ten to the dozen and if left unchecked it would not be unusual to feel more anxious and jittery for some time after this incident. This can be for several reasons not just that your system has been fired up but then we have a tendency to ruminate over what "might" have happened had we not seen the bus and before we know it we have imagined a hospital visit or worse still death. Our thoughts can hijack us at times and feed our threat system with all sorts of perceived dangers. This is why we often find ourselves feeling anxious at times when nothing has necessarily happened at that moment. It's like having an anxiety hangover.

However, if we breathe correctly we can help our vagus nerve activate our parasympathetic system which supports our whole body to settle far quicker. Also, whilst we are focusing on our breath we are not ruminating in our minds, so it's a bit of a double whammy when we use mindful breathing.

There are many free apps that can be downloaded which will talk you through deep breathing. If however, you are happy to breathe independently without a guide, practice the following:

- Breathe in through your nose for the count of three and out through your mouth for the count of three (this can be increased to four and four).
- For a deeper and more impactful breath,

breathe in through your nose for the count of three and out through your mouth for the count of six (this can also be increased to four and eight) so the out-breath is double the in-breath.

Time Management

Time can feel like it is in short supply as a parent, and as a result, this can lead to immense stress when we are trying to juggle all the balls. Then, when an unpredictable factor presents itself, we drop all the balls. Please try not to overcommit, whether that be to multiple after-school clubs or maybe social commitments. Be realistic about what is possible. Remember that you matter too, and working, running a home, and raising children takes time, so limit the number of after-school and social commitments that you and your children have.

26) Waking Up

Ensure that you and your child have a regular time to wake up. I recommend that you try to set your alarm for 20 minutes or half an hour before your child so that you have some quiet time to wake up and have your first cuppa. This may feel counter-intuitive if you've had a broken night's sleep. However, this will likely set you up for the day far better than waking to energetic little people when you're half asleep. This is not always possible with young children who wake up super early, but bear this in mind when they start to sleep a little later.

27) Create A Routine

Establishing a daily routine can bring a sense of structure and calm to both you and your children. If you have nursery or school runs to manage, having a predictable rhythm to your day can be a game-changer. Children naturally gravitate towards predictability, it helps them feel secure and know what's coming next.

By creating a consistent routine, you're not just setting times and places; you're helping your children develop habits that become second nature. While this doesn't mean everything will run smoothly all the time (because, let's face it, who's ever on time ALL the time?), knowing what's expected of them can significantly reduce daily struggles. Kids thrive when they have a sense of what to expect, and a routine provides just that.

28) FREE DAYS

Everyone needs to rest, recharge, and have days with little structure. So, ensure that you and your children have structure-free days such as the weekends. This shows your children that you too need to rest, and they may also appreciate the lack of time constraints that come with daily life during the week. This also helps children not to expect to be busy all of the time. Many parents have shared with me that their children constantly want to be entertained and go out on weekends, whereas the parent is exhausted after a busy week. This is likely because this is what they have always done; therefore, children feel that they are missing out on something if parents dare to say they are having a day at home. Either way, do what is right for you and your family, and create the routine that works for you. Creating a free day can also be a part of your routine.

29) Plan Ahead

If you have busy weeks and quieter weekends, plan the week ahead and prepare meals. Consider batch cooking and freezing. Ensure your and the children's clothes are ready for the week. Schedule drop-offs and pick-ups to school, nursery, and after-school clubs so everybody knows what they are doing. Plan as much in advance as possible to mitigate any unnecessary day-to-day stresses.

30) Use A Calendar

Keep a family calendar to track appointments, activities, and deadlines. Digital calendars are a great way for you and your partner (and older children) to share important events individually and as a family so that everybody can keep abreast of who is doing what and when.

31) Expect Things To Take Longer

Children have very little concept of time, and although it's important to teach them to be punctual, it is also important to aid their development by giving them time to complete tasks that they feel ready to do. For example, your two-year-old may want to put their socks on but can't work out which way up they go or which way around. Give them time to navigate this for themselves. Small challenges such as this build their confidence, self-esteem, and sense of achievement, which is vital in the early years, even though it's so much quicker if you do it; this helps to build their independence, which is what every human wants at the earliest age-appropriate opportunity. Stress can often be created because we have too much to do in too little time. Create space to be flexible; this will make your and your child's experiences so much calmer and more enjoyable.

32) PRACTICE FLEXIBILITY

Expect the unexpected and see every challenge as an opportunity. Children are unpredictable by nature. They get colds or are sick. They suddenly don't want to attend school or do that after-school activity. Therefore, to navigate this path you, and they need time to determine why this might be. Be prepared to be flexible with your time and expectations. When you brought little people into your world, they didn't sign a contract to say that they would seamlessly slot into your world and expectations, so give them time. This will pay dividends in the future because when we are present with our children and give them the space, we are more able to see the world through their eyes and this helps build an incredible bond, trust, and respect between you both.

Parenting Strategies

Navigating being a parent when leading a busy life can feel like an uphill struggle. But I want you to know that it doesn't have to be that way.

Remember that your child is simply a child, and what you feed them, whether that be food, life lessons, or how people manage their emotions, will produce results. Let's look at an example. If you feed your child McDonald's three times a day, seven days a week, there is a good chance your child will not thrive physically, emotionally or psychologically, and it could be really detrimental to their physical health.

As parents, we must pay attention to what we feed our children emotionally, psychologically, and physically. Our children observe the way we think, behave, speak, and feel, and as a result, they pick up what is deemed as 'normal' because the people they hold in natural admiration (which is you) in the early years teach them everything they need to know about how to be a human. Understanding ourselves is fundamental to raising our children and setting them up for success because you are their greatest influencer (who knew that you might not have a million followers on Instagram, but you are somebody's influencer). Let's look at some core strategies you can implement as a parent so that your home is calmer — not only now but in the longer term — even through those pesky teenage years.

Some of these strategies may feel like they take more time. However, like anything, if we invest early on, this pays dividends later in life, and this is no truer than on our parenting journey. So, although you may not see the results related to reducing your stress levels right now, they are likely to prevent unnecessary conflict and reduce potential stress in the future.

33) SET CONSISTENT RULES AND BOUNDARIES

Establish clear and consistent rules and expectations for your children. Life is full of explicit and implicit rules, so teaching our children about rules is important, but we have to remember that humans innately do not like being controlled unnecessarily and ill-thought-through rules can create conflict, so we have to think very carefully about family rules and ensure that they are not simply about us taking control but that there is some value to our child in the longer term. Rules need to be explained clearly and concisely, and they also need to make sense. If children feel they are being controlled and it doesn't make sense to them, as soon as they are of an age where they can kick against the rules, they are likely to. So, I want you to think really carefully about these rules and ensure that they are centred around how they will benefit your child in the longer term, not necessarily as a result of what you want from them or how you were expected to behave as a child.

Consider the following questions when you are implementing rules:

Why am I implementing this rule?

Is this a rule that was implemented in my childhood?

If so, did it make sense to you as a child?

How did you feel about this rule?

What did this rule teach you?

What is this rule teaching my child?

Do I follow my own rules? i.e. You must not lie, you must always be kind.

How will this rule benefit my child in the future?

Am I able to communicate why this rule is important in a way that makes sense to my child?

Rules are a great way to help children navigate the world. The more they can make sense of rules, the more likely they will be to adopt them and follow them because they want to, not just because they have been told to. This also helps breed respect and trust.

Also, try to remain open-minded about flexing on rules. For example, 'You must eat your greens because they are good for you.' If they don't like greens (after all, who does as a child as their palates are very different to ours), then help them find vegetables that they can get on board with, even if they are not their favourite type of food. This provides children with the power of choice and also shows them that you're open to compromise.

34) USE POSITIVE REINFORCEMENT

Encourage positive behaviour with praise. Everybody likes to hear positive feedback. Ensure you acknowledge your child for their achievements, even the smallest ones.

35) RESPECT

Respect and fear can often be confused. Respect is something that is earned, not commanded.

Let's begin by examining how fear can sometimes be mistaken for respect. True respect is not earned by instilling a fear of consequences. We often see a child who is 'conforming' as being respectful. However, it's important to recognise that you do not want your child to conform out of fear of consequences. These consequences may not always be overt; for instance, children really dislike disappointing their parents, so the fear of disappointment may lead them to conform. While conforming in certain areas of life is important, if a child learns that they will only be approved of or liked if they conform, it could lead them to take this mindset into all relationships, potentially making them 'people pleasers'. As parents, we want our children to feel that they have a voice and can articulate their views and opinions in adult life without fearing rejection. It's important that if your child occasionally resists your authority, you see this as a learning opportunity.

If your child doesn't do as they are told it doesn't necessarily mean they don't respect you; it simply means they are human. Firstly, nobody likes being told what to do, so crafting your requests so that your child is more likely to receive and respond favourably should be your aim. For example: "I would really appreciate it if you could tidy your room today" versus "Go and tidy your room NOW." The first example is respectful and calm, while the second is dictatorial and potentially disrespectful. If we want our children to respect us, we must respect them.

When your child speaks to you in a way that feels off or disrespectful (which they will), remember that each situation and child is unique, so firstly don't compare one child to another. It's sometimes easy to say, "Why can't you behave as your sister does". Remember each child is unique and brings a whole unique set of challenges and joys with them.

It's important to keep in mind that children's brains aren't yet fully equipped to regulate their emotional responses. This ability develops over time and is a natural part of growing up. It's not an excuse for poor behaviour, but an understanding of where they are in their emotional journey.

Even many adults struggle with regulating their emotions, so it's no surprise that children, whose brains are still developing, may have intense emotional reactions and what may seem benign to us can feel overwhelming to them, resulting in what looks like disrespect but is often just an unfiltered expression of their emotions.

Supporting children in learning to manage their emotions takes patience and empathy. It's essential to stay calm and regulated yourself when your child is having an emotional moment.

If you react emotionally to their outburst, you both become dysregulated, which rarely leads to a positive outcome.

If they speak to you disrespectfully, you might say something like, "I don't appreciate being spoken to in that way; I'm happy to help resolve X, but let's do it together calmly." Once your child's emotions have settled, having a chat with them about how they spoke to you is important so they understand that you have personal boundaries and will not accept being spoken to in a way that feels disrespectful to you, even if that is not their intention. Exploring what upset them also gives them the opportunity to feel heard and understood. The likelihood of your child feeling bad about how they spoke to you is quite high, so make sure, when things are calm, that you draw a line under the experience and move on. This shows your child that you will not hold a grudge, and as a result, respect builds.

But the question remains, how do I earn my child's respect?

Think of someone you respect:

Why do you respect them?

What did they do to earn your respect?

Respect is often not instantaneous. It usually takes time to respect someone, with multiple examples of behaviour that earn your respect.

Now apply this to your child:

What are you doing to earn their respect?

Are you modelling respectful behaviour not only to them but in every area of your life?

Are you consistent? Are you largely predictable?

Respect is a cornerstone of a strong bond with your child, so fostering boundaries and encouraging respectful behaviour by modelling it yourself will set the foundations for your relationship to flourish.

36) POWER AND CONTROL

"Your child will only allow you to have power until they decide to take it back."

Ouch... what does that mean? Well, children have to relinquish their power in their formative years because they simply cannot navigate the world alone. How we, as parents, use that power is crucial, because every human being wants their own power, and in order to thrive in life, we must have some power and control over our lives. Use your power wisely. Don't abuse your power by controlling your child. Allow them age-appropriate control. This will differ for every child, but remember, you brought them into this world to become thriving human beings so slowly introducing them to age-appropriate independence, and supporting their emotional growth by listening to their views, opinions, and thoughts, helps them immensely in adult life when they are likely to face many challenges. If a child has been overly controlled in their infancy and adolescence, they may allow themselves to be controlled, or they could become controlling themselves in future relationships. Balance is essential for thriving relationships, so teach them the importance of balance with power and control.

37) STAY CALM

Practice staying calm and composed during challenging situations. Remember that your emotions are yours, and your child's emotions are theirs. Separate how you feel from how your child feels and support your child when they are dysregulated. If you become dysregulated, it can simply breed additional stress. Nobody likes it when their child is struggling emotionally, and this can leave us feeling as though we are failing in some way. Try not to go there. Children, like all human beings, have fluctuating emotions. This is normal. It's about how we manage them. Stay calm and breathe.

38) COMMUNICATION

How we communicate is key to building strong relationships, there isn't a single parent who hasn't shouted at or missed what their child was saying because they were busy and stressed. Remember that you are a fallible human, and you are unlikely to be present and calm all the time. But communicating respectfully and being fully present 'most' of the time will go a long way to building a lovely, strong bond and fostering respect. When we have children, we expect them to respect us. This is not something children are born with. We all need to earn respect from one another, and that respect comes in multiple forms. Consider the following:

- Ensure you speak to your child in the way you would like to be spoken to. Your child is watching how you communicate with them, how you speak about yourself, and how you speak to your partner and others. Remember that you are modelling how to be a human being, and they are likely to copy you. Rest assured, no one instance of shouting or disrespect will embed itself into your child's belief system. We simply need to communicate respectfully MOST of the time.

- If you consistently shout because you don't feel heard (so essentially, your emotions have been triggered), your child will likely adopt the same method and shout. They will not see this as disrespectful, simply that this is the norm and how people communicate. Unfortunately, this can also lead to them waiting until you shout before they actually register that you're speaking.

- Pause, If you feel frustration building and you're likely to say something in a way that could cause conflict, take a breath. This will calm your nervous system and give you an opportunity to say what's needed calmly.

- Be mindful of how you talk about yourself too. If you are self-critical, this could give your child, or others, permission to be critical of you too, and they may also pick up this trait and become hypercritical of themselves.

39) SUPPORT PROBLEM-SOLVING

Help your children develop problem-solving skills. As parents, we often want to support our children so much that we do things for them because we don't like to see them struggle. However, activating the part of their brain that influences problem-solving is a great way to stretch their minds in an age-appropriate way. For example, if your two-year-old is struggling to figure out which way round their sock goes on their foot, help them to work it out. You could say something like:

"Let's find where your toes go, and now let's see where your heel goes. Which way round do you think you need to put your foot into the sock?"

This is a very simple example, but the more

children are encouraged to problem-solve, the stronger this ability becomes. In adulthood, they are more likely to be able to tackle complex tasks. Remember, you are not just parenting for today; you are parenting for the years to come. So, although taking the time to help children problem-solve may be challenging in your busy life, this will pay dividends as they grow older because they will learn to rely on you less and on themselves more.

40) Foster Independence

Encourage your children to do things on their own to build confidence, but do so in an age-appropriate way. Children should not be given too much independence where it may cause them harm, and there is no one-size-fits-all approach. Your child is unique, so help them progress at the speed of their development, not at the pace of their friends or your friends' children or indeed your own experience of childhood.

Children often 'want' more independence ahead of time. For example, they may not understand why they can't go to the park with their older sibling when they are still young.

Remember, they may see their sibling as super mature and therefore responsible. They may also witness their older sibling having independence. It's important to explain to your child the real reasons why this isn't possible. You might say something like:

"You may not fully understand this, but it's really important for me to keep you safe. I've spent a few years teaching your sibling how to be safe at the park with their friends, and you and I will also do this together. But for now, I don't want you to go to the park without me. How about I come with you, and I will sit a little distance away so that I can see that you're safe, but you can play with your friends?"

Negotiating with children and compromising is crucial for them to feel that they have some control over their lives, but not too much. Remember, children thrive when they feel safe, so although they may 'want' to go to the park with the older kids, that doesn't always mean they will feel safe when they get there. This is something we, as parents, must navigate.

Did your parents encourage age-appropriate independence in you as a child? Or did you feel you had too much or too little freedom to choose?

How we were raised can subtly influence our expectations of our children. Noting your experience as a child can be really valuable.

41) CREATE A CALM ENVIRONMENT

VOCAL NOISE

Where possible, create a calm and peaceful environment. Children and babies struggle to thrive in environments where unpredictable and uncertain behaviour from the people around them occurs. This can be anything from frequent shouting, aggression, and violence to a key parent figure being emotionally unavailable, which can be a result of their own unresolved emotional challenges.

People often think that babies are not impacted or will not remember the early years, as few of us remember under the age of 3 or 4. Sadly, if we are exposed to unpredictable behaviour frequently, although we may not have specific logical memories, we now know that this can impact the activation of a baby's threat system (the Amygdala) prematurely and, as a result, begins to set the stage for their vulnerability to anxiety, stress and mental health struggles in the future. It is also widely documented that we store emotional memories within our bodies. Bessel Van De Kolk published an incredible book which focuses on this specific subject, "The Body Keeps The Score".

Although this sounds a little scary, it is important to acknowledge that this is not the case if there are minor hiccups or rare unpredictability; this is mainly if the child is exposed to regular episodes. However, this shows that a child's environment impacts how they evolve emotionally. Communicating respectfully and calmly is important not only for children to feel safe in their environment but also to model how to resolve conflict in a healthy way, which is essential in adult life.

This may be a good time for some reflection on how your childhood was!

Was it calm?

Was there regular friction?

Or was there a balance, or maybe a few tricky times?

Did you largely feel emotionally safe in your home?

Were you anxious around one or both of your parents?

Understanding the part our childhood home plays in how we now manage our emotions can provide us with true insight into why we are the people we are today and also provide us with a platform for our own parenting journey.

Visual Noise

Of course, when we think about our environment we often do not consider the part that visual noise may play on our wellbeing. Some people like visual noise, such as a whole wall filled with bookshelves and multi-coloured books on them. For others, this can be overwhelming. To be honest I'm not entirely sure young children really consider visual noise too much, although this can be a challenge for older children. However if as adults we struggle with organising our homes, this can contribute to what should be our sanctuary being a place of dread and stress, which can again add to the ever-increasing layers of contributing factors that culminate into feeling stressed.

People often do not feel relaxed in an untidy environment, as the brain can see that there are many jobs to do but we often don't know where to start. For others, visual noise is commonplace in their lives and although it is not something they enjoy there is likely to be an underlying reason as to why the visual noise exists in their homes. Personally, I find that I clean and tidy more if I am feeling overloaded in other areas of my life, as a tidy house helps my mind to feel tidy. Often, I may not even realise I'm overloaded until I find myself tidying.

Ask yourself the following questions:

Do you like a tidy home, or do you have a lot of visual noise in your home?

Does your home emulate your childhood home in any way, or perhaps the opposite?

How do you feel about your home?

How do other family members feel about your home?

Depending on how you have answered these questions, this may have piqued some curiosity as to changes that you may or may not want to make. And If you struggle with staying on top of the domesticity of life and you prefer a tidy home then I'm coming back to the idea of hiring a cleaner or maybe even investing in an "organiser"! I recognise this may come at a cost that you can ill afford, but it's exactly these sorts of investments that we may need to make to reduce the on going drip drip drip of our emotional energy because the bathroom needs cleaning AGAIN. Such support is likely to be far cheaper than a therapist when all the moving parts come to a head in life. Mitigate as much stress in your life as possible and outsource where possible. If visual noise drives you mad, talk to your family about it and share with them that this isn't about you being particular but that it actually creates a stress response for you, and could they help you to manage that? However, also be open to not sweating the small stuff and accepting that when we share a home with others the environment is not likely to be able to be exactly as we would like.

I will share an example with you. Prior to becoming a dog mum, everything doggie would drive me nuts. The idea of hair on my clothes and picking up dog poop was a trigger for me. However, everybody within my family apart from me was super keen to get a dog, so a dog we got. Initially, the constant dog hair did drive me a little crazy but now I just let it go. Poppy is a much-loved part of our family and as a result, her moulting hair comes with her, along with the fact that the living room constantly looks like we have a toddler in the house due to her ever-growing basket of toys (yep, I buy them) and I wouldn't have it any other way. So now I don't sweat the small stuff. I just accept that I love our pooch and that far outweighs the things that once upon a time I would have struggled with. It's safe to say she has become my dog, even though I was the one who had the doubts. So sometimes identifying why something triggers us and working through that can be really empowering.

It's also always good to see how family members feel about visual noise too, to get a gauge on the impact on them. I remember one of my children saying, as they got older, how they needed to tidy their bedroom because it was stressing them out. Even young people can get stressed with visual noise (and they may not even know it). If this is the case for your child and they need help knowing where to start, then support them with this. But be mindful that this isn't about you satisfying your need for tidiness; it's about helping them feel better in their own space. You might say something like:

"I don't mind how your bedroom looks, but I'm happy to help you if you need guidance on where to start."

Conversely, they may be quite happy in their untidy bedroom. If so, try and let it be. This is their space, and especially as they become teenagers, they do not want a parent messing with their space (in fact, I recommend that you gain permission from them to enter their space, as this shows that you respect their privacy). Provide them with the respect they want but let them know that you are there to help them if they need it.

Exploring all areas of our lives can be valuable

in mitigating the build-up of stress. We live much of our lives subconsciously and may not even consider things such as 'visual noise'. However, if you can make small tweaks in various areas of your life that reduce your stress and anxiety, this will have a compound effect overall.

42) MODELLING

Demonstrate the behaviour you wish to see in your children. Remember what I mentioned earlier, children watch us and copy us. Everything you do, say, the way you behave, your passions, your hobbies, and how you cope with your emotions, is being picked up by your child. Some of this they will ignore, but other aspects they will embrace and copy. Unfortunately, we cannot predict the things they will repeat and the things they won't, so ensure that you are modelling healthy behaviour that you would be happy for your child to copy.

If your child is exhibiting a behaviour that you don't appreciate, consider whether someone significant to them may be demonstrating such behaviour. This is not to say that, for example, when you are distressed, you will throw a complete fit in Tesco's, because we must allow space for the fact that children's emotions are naturally dysregulated, but let's say, for example, you find yourself shouting more frequently than you would like, and something that drives you nuts is that your child communicates in a similar way. The best way to reduce this behaviour is to model a different behaviour. So, for example, rather than shouting, you might explain calmly that you are not happy with X, Y, or Z. This is not always easy, but teaching through modelling is far more powerful than simply telling a child how to behave. Equally, if we tell a child not to do something that we do ourselves, this makes no sense to them, and as we know, children like things to make sense.

43) Accountability And Consequences

'Punishment' can be a tricky subject for parents as not only do we not want our children to do things that warrant punishment, but it never feels good when we deliver a punishment. For me, accountability and consequences are the route to growth and learning.

Let me set out an example for you. A common challenge I hear from many parents is when they have given their child a certain amount of screen time, and the child rebels and argues about wanting more screen time when it's time to turn their device off. This can often lead to conflict. Then, at the point where both parent and child are frustrated and essentially emotionally dysregulated, the parent might ban the child from screen time for a week. Eeeeek!! Then, because the punishment was delivered in the heat of the moment, the parent may regret how long they have put the ban in place and either spend the next week being badgered by their child because they are bored, or they may retract their initial punishment and reduce the time frame.

In a situation like this, the child may learn several things:

- If they don't conform, they will be punished harshly.
- They may feel powerless in their efforts.
- Parents make the rules up as they go along and can pull a punishment out of anywhere, and there is nothing they can do.

- You're mean.
- If they ask enough times, they may get the punishment reduced.

This is not to say that you shouldn't have rules and boundaries, as we know children thrive on boundaries. But it's about how you execute them to reduce the chances of conflict.

If you have noticed a pattern in your child's behaviour where they rebel or display actions that you want to help them manage, talk to them about it when everything is calm, and both you and your child are relaxed. For example, you might say something like:

You: "Let's have a chat about how you feel when your screen time is coming to an end. Why do you think you get so upset when it's time to come off your device?"

Your child: "It's just not enough time, and I was right in the middle of something, and if I stopped, I would lose everything I had done."

You: "Okay, so let's find a way to resolve this, because it's not nice for you or me when situations like that happen. So, how much time would you like a day for screen time?"

Your child: "I would like an extra half an

hour."

You: "Well, half an hour extra means it will be too much screen time for one day, so how about we compromise, and you can have an extra 15 minutes?

Your child: "That sounds good; an extra 15 minutes would be great."

You: However, we also need to talk about what happens if you get upset even though you have an extra 15 minutes. I don't want to be falling out with you over anything, especially not screen time, so how about I remind you when you have 15 minutes left on your screen, and then you can start finishing off what you are doing and get to a point where you can save your game?"

Your child: "That would be good, or maybe I could set an alarm for 15 mins before"

You: "That's a great idea. So let's talk about what will happen if you don't come off when your time is up."

Your child: "Well, I hate it when you ban me from my device, as I really enjoy it."

You: "And I understand that, and I don't like banning it, but there is a good reason I limit your screen time, and that is because too much is not good for your developing brain. So, we need to find a consequence together if you don't come off when your time is up. Although I think going forward, we won't need a consequence because I'm sure you will, as I know you don't like falling out either, do you? So, what do you think the consequence should be?"

Your child: "I don't know… Maybe three days? I hate it when it's a week—that's just like forever."

You: "Okay, how about we say we take your screen time away for one day? How does that sound?"

Your child: "OK" (they're probably thinking, 'what's the catch?').

You: "There is something that I want you to remember now that we have decided on this together. You have agreed that if you don't come off your screen in time, then you are choosing to lose your device for a day? This isn't me being mean or unkind; it is simply something we have agreed upon together. How does that sound?"

Your child: "That sounds okay. I will come off in time."

What does this teach your child?

- The art of compromise.
- That they are responsible for the consequence, not you.
- This is predictable because it has been discussed and agreed upon.
- They had some control over the outcome.
- Because this is in place, you are less likely to get frustrated and will simply implement the consequence with ease, maybe saying something like, "Remember the discussion we had? We agreed together that this would be the consequence if you chose not to come off your device in the allotted time."

Your child is likely to come off much calmer. They may be sad and disappointed, but they are likely to accept what has happened and move on.

The more consistent you are with your efforts, the more your child will trust the process and therefore see that they have a choice as to whether they receive consequences, rather than you being the 'bad guy' for punishing them.

A final point on this: do not multi-layer. Another common mistake we have all made is:

"That's it—you've now lost it for another

day because you've been rude, and another, and another!"

Don't do this. Expect your child to be upset that you are implementing the consequence, but don't punish them for being upset. Validate their frustration or sadness. Keep reminding them that it was a choice they made. In time, they will learn that they really do have a choice and will likely start to make the right choices for themselves.

There is nothing more stressful than trying to navigate conflict with your child. So, to reduce your stress, implement clear, concise, and reasonable boundaries. This will help both you and your relationship.

Strengthening Your Bond

44) Schedule Quality Time

Set aside 'protected time' for each child to strengthen your bond. When they know they have some one-on-one time with you, they are less likely to be constantly vying for your attention. Children are often reasonable when they know their needs will be met, and of course they want to spend time with you. The stress that can build for parents because they feel guilty for not giving their child the attention they want, due to life's demands, can be huge. So, create 'protected time' with your child, and if you have more than one child, create specific time for each one. This will vastly reduce the time you spend not only trying to quieten that negative internal chatter but also the number of times you find yourself saying, 'Yes, I will be there in a minute,' or fire-fighting the latest challenge. Children want to be seen. I still seek opportunities to have protected time with my children, and they are now adults, even if its going to the supermarket together. This provides an opportunity to reconnect away from other stressors in life. Here are a few tips on creating protected time:

• **How much time should I protect?**

This doesn't have to be hours or a whole day. Just some specific time for the two of you. It may be reading a book together or a whole day out. Either way, any time is important time.

• **What should I do with my child?**

Choose something together, but I encourage you to do something they enjoy, even if it's not something you really want to do. Reap the joy of watching them immerse themselves in sharing with you what lights them up.

• **If you have a teenager (or at any age, really)**

Ask them if they can show you or teach you more about their latest passion, whether it be an Xbox game, a craft, or maybe their favourite programme, essentially, whatever it is they like to do in their spare time. Children LOVE teaching us adults a thing or two.

45) AFFECTION

Affection can feel tricky if you're not a touchy-feely person. Perhaps your parents didn't overtly tell you they loved you, so it doesn't come naturally to you as your parents modelled that this is not something we do as humans. OR it may be that you are determined for your child to have a different experience but question whether you are showering your child with too much love. No child can be loved too much but sometimes if our needs have not been met in childhood, we find it really difficult to feel confident that we are meeting our child's needs effectively and constantly keep an eye out for feedback from them which can breed anxiety in us as parents, which our children pick up on.

Overtly expressing love and affection helps build a bond and strengthen relationships, whether that be with your partner or children. When we share a cuddle with another person, our brain releases the 'Love Hormone,' oxytocin, into the bloodstream, which reduces cortisol levels and lowers blood pressure. What better way to reduce stress levels than a quick cuddle (although the longer the cuddle, the better—10 seconds or more is perfect).

Many children know they are loved by a parent's actions, but please, please, please tell and show your children and partner that you love them. This reduces any ambiguity and provides them with the knowledge that they are safe and secure within the relationship.

46) LISTEN ACTIVELY

Practise active listening to understand your children's needs and concerns. How many times have you heard your child, your partner, or a colleague speaking, and you've pretty much picked up what they are saying and are able to respond, but you're not really listening? This is a common human flaw when we are busy. However, have you ever been speaking to someone and you know they are not listening. How does that feel? Well, often we don't feel heard, which can lead to frustration and even stress. Ensure that when someone is speaking to you, especially your child, you try to stop what you're doing and focus on what they are saying. I acknowledge that children are usually chattering ten to the dozen constantly, so you may not always be able to stop what you're doing, but if this is the case, then ask them to wait a moment while you finish what you're doing, then take a pause and ask them to repeat what they have said. 93% of communication is non-verbal. Only 7% of communication consists of the words that come out of our mouths. So, to get a sense of what someone is saying, we have to listen to the words, their voice tone, and observe their body language. We can't do all of those things if we're busy doing something else. This is where telephone conversations, texts, and emails can cause problems because we may only have a person's words, and with the absence of all the other important aspects of communication, these messages can be misunderstood and misinterpreted. If you take the time to 'listen' to your child, you will find they are less likely to repeat the same thing over and over because, although they are children, if they sense you are not listening, they may repeat themselves until you do listen.

47) Say YES More Than NO

This may seem like a contradiction to the 'boundaries' section. Maintaining boundaries is really important in all areas of life, but often as parents, we may say NO for reasons other than boundary setting. Has your child ever asked you if they can do something, and straightaway, it's a NO, whether that be because you are trying to protect your child or perhaps because it's inconvenient? Before you say YES or NO, think carefully about your reason why. If something scares you, let's say, for example, your child wants to climb a tree. Of course, you are going to fear for their safety, but saying YES and putting your fears aside and helping them to climb the tree safely supports your child in exploring areas that they are curious about. This will also send them the message that you believe in them, which can help to build high self-esteem. If we don't believe in our children, they learn not to believe in themselves (we are definitely influencers in this area). Saying NO can create more curiosity, and they are more likely to attempt climbing the tree when you are not around to tell them no, but they may not be able to do this safely and are more likely to fall out of the tree. As parents, we have the capacity to educate our children about navigating this world, but if we focus on our fears rather than their desires, it doesn't mean they won't explore, they just won't share that exploration with us. Ask yourself the question, "Were there things you did in childhood that you didn't share with your parents because you knew they would say no?"

Young people don't necessarily want permission; they want guidance. Children and teenagers often do not see the dangers in many things, this is due to their neurological development. The conscious, logical, reasoning part of the brain isn't initially connected to the risk-taking impulsive part of the brain. This fusion starts to take place at the age of 13 and completes age 25 (I can hear you saying 'Whhaaatttt') Yep…. Have a think about all the decisions you made pre-25, the chances are most of the mistakes you made that make you cringe now were in this age group. Now you know why.

So, helping them identify risks, supports the development of this part of their brain, and even if something is deemed risky, if you are supporting them and talking with them about the risks and benefits and potential outcomes, this will help them assess things more effectively in the future.

The more you say YES and support your child, the more powerful the NO becomes when it is essential, and they are less likely to question it because they trust that the NO is for a valid and reasonable reason. When my son was 16 years old I found myself in exactly this situation where I had collaborated with him and said yes more than no throughout his younger years and on this day he came home from school and presented with a request that sent a ripple of fear down my spine and at this point I knew this was going to be the test as to whether my theory was right, that when I did say no, would he respect it and conform to it and he did, he just agreed, just like that. I had a solid justification for my HARD NO, however, what struck me was he didn't even argue it or ask for an explanation, it was like he instantly accepted and respected that if I were saying no then there was a good reason and he didn't need to question it. Just for context, I have always given my children a voice and heard them and emulated everything I advocate for and sometimes as a parent that feels like it bites you a little because then you have children that question and debate, which can be challenging albeit this is great as they grow and evolve. So this young man questions most things but on this day he didn't feel the need to, he just accepted it.

Where possible If you do have to say NO, then explaining why it is a NO is also extremely important. 'Because I said so' is not an explanation. Building trust and respect with children is essential, and although young children are essentially within our control, this is only for a short period before they start to flex their independence. Guiding them early on will pay dividends for when they are teenagers and adults alike because they trust you to put their needs and wants first.

48) ENCOURAGE OPEN COMMUNICATION

Create an environment where your children feel safe to express themselves. This can be challenging, especially when your child becomes a teenager and shares things that you might prefer not to hear. But trust me when I say that if you create an environment that encourages open and honest communication, you will have the opportunity to support, educate, and help your child to grow. Open communication reduces the desire for children to keep secrets and tell untruths because they learn to trust that, as their parent, they can tell you anything and you will guide them in the best way possible.

49) Practice Patience

Be patient and understanding with your children's growth and development. Patience can feel in limited supply when we are busy parents, and often as adults, we don't understand why a child doesn't just follow the instructions to do what we require of them. Remember, children are not working on our timeframe, nor are they as able to understand and think things through in the way we can because their brains simply aren't developed sufficiently to navigate the complexities of life. Slowing everything down will enable you to foster more patience when your child is on their steep learning curve of life. Children's brains are absorbing so much information in their early years; it's a bit like infant university, most of which doesn't make sense to them. Our patience is often stretched when we are too busy and under pressure. Identify areas where you can alleviate some of that pressure, as this action alone will help to calm your system and foster more patience.

50) REPAIR

Remember that being a parent is not about being perfect, and naturally, when life challenges us from multiple angles, there will be times when you make mistakes, do things you wish you hadn't done, or say things you wish you hadn't said, or perhaps your child has overheard.

Teaching children how to repair is really important.

- **Apologise:** If you have made a mistake, then apologise. Your child will accept this, and it will also teach them that getting things wrong is okay as long as we apologise and learn from it.
- **Reconnect**: If your child has done something wrong, reconnect with them as soon as possible. This could be chatting with them,

being curious about what they are doing, or maybe you simply want to give them a hug. This helps children know that you have moved on and so can they.

- **Silent treatment**: Don't give them the silent treatment. Once the issue is resolved, move on. The silent treatment leaves children feeling on edge, and they may become desperate to get back on your good side. This is a sign that they are uncomfortable with your disapproval, and this is simply a form of punishment.

- **Let it go**: Don't keep reminding them of 'when' they did something wrong. Draw a line under it and move on.

- **Repeating it**: Try not to tell others about what happened within earshot of your child. This feels shaming to them. If you need to share it with their other parent, make sure this is done privately. Modelling that you have let it go, but then continuing to bring it up, sends very mixed messages.

Repair is so important for any relationship to thrive. This doesn't mean that you have to apologise even if you're not in the wrong; it's simply about identifying the part you may have played, and if for any reason your child or partner is not ready to resolve the situation, then give them some time and space and come back to it. Unresolved frustration and anger can fester, so ensure that you do return to it and resolve the situation calmly.

Bonus Section: Partner Relationships

You may have found that your relationship has changed since having children, and if all is going well, your relationship may be thriving. Or you may have encountered a few bumps in the road. Right now, you may need all the support you can get, yet with the little energy you have, you may feel you certainly don't have enough to invest in your relationship, and you may be thinking, 'It's okay, we will get through this, this is normal family life'. Everything in life requires investment and maintenance, and our relationships are no different. The divorce rates for mid-life are soaring, and in my experience, this is largely due to the inadvertent neglect of the relationship that is the bedrock of our families in the hope that it will be okay. Your relationship deserves much more than that.

We all need a soft place to land, and what better place than with the life partner you chose? Taking care of your relationship is important to ensure you continue growing together.

You Have Both Changed

Firstly, I just want to acknowledge the fact that you have both changed and you will continue to change, as will your relationship. It is important to accept that there will be things you miss about your former life before children. This is absolutely fine; it doesn't mean anything other than a natural transitional stage when settling into parenthood. However, it is okay to miss what you had, and the feeling of loss will slowly dissipate over time. If you have been a parent for a while, you may recognise this stage of parenting.

Remember Why You Chose Your Partner

Never forget why you chose your partner. There will be incredible things about them that you really appreciated, some of which may have changed, and others that may have emerged throughout your time together. Remind yourself daily of why you chose this person. Sometimes we can become complacent within our relationships, and my message to you is: never become complacent. I have seen far too many people coming for therapy when they have already checked out of the relationship, and they didn't see it coming. Nurture your relationship every day and remind yourself why you chose each other TODAY.

ARE YOU ON THE SAME PARENTING PAGE?

This can be super tricky. You chose your partner for being who they are. However, now that you are both parents, you may find yourself getting frustrated because they don't appear to have stepped up to the role, or you are finding that you have to 'ask' them to do things that surely they should just know to do.

I cannot emphasise enough how important it is for you both to be on the same page as parents, or at the very least in the same book. Not only does this create an amazing foundation for your child to thrive, but also for your relationship. If you are in constant conflict or even silent conflict about how your children should be parented, this may erode your relationship.

We know that when choosing a partner, we as human beings look for familiarity, often without realising it. We are drawn to certain types of people and may even notice a pattern of choosing the same type of person, with the relationships ending in similar ways. Yet, we are drawn to another version of that person the next time.

This is because we are subliminally drawn to a partner who symbolises our mother or father. For example, you may notice traits of one of your parents in yourself, and you will likely see traits of your other parent in your partner. This is normal and far from weird. It is human nature. We are drawn to familiar behaviours, attitudes, and beliefs that have been bred in us through observing our parents. On the flip side, you too may symbolise one of your partner's parents, and they the other.

How each of you was raised has a fundamental influence on how you raise your children, and so much of our parenting programming silently lives in our subconscious. This has not only been passed down from our parents, grandparents, and great-grandparents but also from your partner's family line too. Then, as a couple, you are trying to raise your beautiful family with all these opposing views. Is it any surprise so many couples struggle to be on the same page? If you are finding that you have different parenting views, beliefs, or behaviours, this will be a result of how you were both raised differently.

Exploring your programming will not only shine a light on how you both align but also where your challenges lie. This can set you on a path to parenting together in a way that not only supports your children's emotional development, decision-making, and mental health but also your relationship. When we are happy and content within our romantic relationship, it can relieve some of the stressors we are experiencing in life because we have that safe place to land. Also, don't forget that oxytocin, which is deemed as the "love hormone" is an incredible stress-buster. Research has found that as little as a six-second cuddle can create an oxytocin release in the brain. Imagine how you would feel with a twenty-second cuddle. If we also go back to our parenting role – every time you cuddle your child they too have a release of oxytocin and not only know they are loved but they 'feel' loved.

COMMUNICATION AND LISTENING

I am going to echo what I have already said in this book.

- Listen to each other without judgement.
- Communicate respectfully.
- Validate each other's experiences and emotions.
- Support each other through challenges.

If, as a couple, you have good communication skills and are respectful of each other's emotions, you will be able to weather any storm.

Communication is at the centre of a healthy relationship. Being able to share how you feel and the potential challenges you are facing within the relationship stops them from festering and building up.

CONFLICT

Conflict tends to ensue when someone does

something that we don't want them to do (so essentially, we experience anger or fear). How we resolve conflict as a couple can stem from our childhoods. This is an area I encourage you to consider because how your parents or your partner's parents resolve or don't resolve conflict may feature in your relationship and, therefore, be playing out in your family home.

- How did your parents resolve conflict?
- Do you react to conflict in a similar way to one of your parents?
- If you do, take yourself back and remind yourself how you felt as a child. Is this how you want your child to feel? (this can be positive or negative)
- How would you like to respond to conflict?

Children, and a vast majority of adults, do not like conflict. Children have very little control over whether they are exposed to conflict, and they certainly cannot remove themselves from the environment entirely to escape it.

Many people suggest that having a good argument is healthy for relationships. I disagree. Nothing good comes from emotions being out of control, where things are said in the heat of the moment as a result of rage and anger. This often leads to regret, guilt, and possibly fear.

When we lose control emotionally to a point where the conflict has escalated, nobody is in control, and children know this and often fear what the outcome might be. Remember that anger is a perfectly normal emotion, but whether we react or respond and how we behave as a result is where it can become unhealthy. Give some thought to how you and family members respond to anger and conflict.

THINGS TO REMEMBER WHEN YOU ARE IN DISAGREEMENT WITH YOUR PARTNER (the main aim being to defuse the situation)

- **Firstly, take a breath:** When we find ourselves in conflict, we often go into survival mode, so our logical brain shuts down, and the survival brain takes over. This is why we may say or do things that are out of character when angry. By taking a breath, you wake up your logical brain so that you can respond to the situation rather than react.
- **Don't defend**: When we start defending

ourselves, this is where conflict tends to erupt. Wait until things have calmed down, then have a calm conversation about your view and opinion.

- **Try to stay calm:** whether your partner or child is dysregulated, remember that your emotions are yours, and theirs are theirs. Multiple people feeling dysregulated creates a perfect storm.
- **Speak in a calm manner, even if your partner is shouting**: They are more likely to calm down if you are calm. Then you can discuss the matter calmly.
- **Validate the emotions of your partner:** Explain that you can see they are angry and you are happy to discuss this calmly when they are ready.

Once everything has calmed down, revisit the situation and discuss what wasn't said and how you could both work towards improving conflict resolution going forward.

Don't Sweep Things Under the Carpet

Often, we tell ourselves, "Don't sweat the small

stuff," and that is true, but if the small stuff is just being pushed away and building up, we are still sweating the small stuff, just quietly. Then, all of a sudden, we go boom, and nobody understands what's happened. This can also be the case if we have been agreeable in a disagreement just to smooth the waters, when in fact, we are still angry, feel unheard, and invalidated.

The moral of the story is, do not sweep anything under the carpet as it will just lay there and go mouldy, and more and more will get swept under the carpet, and then you just have a big mess but no idea how it even got there.

Many relationships suffer as a result of dismissing things, leaving one or both parties feeling hurt or disrespected, and yet they may feel compelled to try and forget it. We do not forget pain; we store it in our bodies and minds, and if we experience repeated instances from the same person, we slowly remove ourselves as a way of protecting ourselves. Then, maybe many years later, we realise that we have very few feelings for that person because we have allowed them to treat us in a certain way, or we have simply let things go to the point where our pain and frustration have created such a mound under the carpet that we can no longer ignore it.

This is why I am saying do not leave things unsaid. Hash it out (respectfully), talk things through, work out where each other is coming from so that you can understand. It is exactly this that builds the foundations of thriving relationships and, therefore, a solid family unit.

Repair

We often don't set out to upset our partners, and sometimes we both may have different ideas about what the relationship rules are. This, again, can stem from our differing relationship styles, which may have been influenced by our parents.

However, if you do experience conflict within your relationship, ensure you work as hard on the repair as you did on the conflict, if not harder. Say sorry, even if you don't think you did anything wrong; say, "I'm sorry my actions left you feeling that way; that wasn't my intention." Essentially, you may not be sorry for the action because it wasn't done with ill intent, but you are sorry your partner feels the way they do.

Find a resolution to ensure this won't happen again. This doesn't mean that because your partner didn't like what you did, you can't do it again; it simply means finding a way to compromise and help each other to see the other's viewpoint.

DATE NIGHT

Always make space for 'couple time'. This doesn't have to be a weekend away or even a night out. If you have little ones and they have a bedtime routine, you may be able to cook dinner together or share a takeaway at the table whilst chatting and listening to music.

Ensure you make time for each other to reconnect. It is all too easy to be super busy and, as a result, very exhausted. Remember, this is the relationship you chose, and you both deserve to create a space where you can provide each other with your undivided attention. It is these kinds of moments that open up the lines of communication if there are any brewing challenges and stop them in their tracks. This is not just a nice-to-have; try to make it a MUST in your diary.

Final Words

This book was written with you in mind, as a whole human being with your many hats. The moral of the story is to take good care of yourself. Nobody knows how exhausted you are or how stressed you are better than you. Nobody can advocate for you better than you. This isn't because people don't care; it's simply because we are all different, and our whole history plays a part in how we cope and manage life's stresses. So, advocate for yourself, be your biggest champion, stand in your corner, and know your limitations.

Check in and remind yourself how many balls you are juggling or hats you are wearing. Does something need to give? What is working well and what isn't?

Remember, if you are feeling the pressures of

life, then everybody benefits in the long term if you give yourself permission to make changes. They may not like the short-term change, but they will adapt.

- What can you change today?
- What can you add to your life that will improve things?
- What can you remove from your life that is holding you back?

At the end of each day, ask yourself,

"What could have made today better?"

Today doesn't end today; it has a ripple effect into the future. The corner we turn today takes us in a different direction than if we had simply taken the next left. Nothing we do stays in today. Ensure that you are working towards what you want in life. Look after your overall wellbeing so that when you are elderly and reflecting on your life, you can appreciate having looked after your body and mind when you were at your busiest because it has meant you can enjoy your twilight years healthy and well. Now, we all know that looking after ourselves doesn't necessarily guarantee our wellbeing in the future. However, you can be fairly certain that if we allow our bodies to suffer the effects of high levels of cortisol for extended periods, it is likely to be far more detrimental than if we learn the art of saying no and put our perfectionist hat down. Because when we are in our twilight years, the need for perfectionism will have passed, and we will know that we were loved by the people we loved, and the rest of the world really didn't matter, and the boss we spent so much time trying to impress—we can no longer remember their name.

Prioritise, plan, have goals, but be realistic and most of all be kind to yourself. Remember, nobody made you the milk police, so let someone else go and get the milk.

About the Author

Nicola Saunders is a psychotherapist with over 20 years of clinical experience, a wife, and a proud mum of two children and a dog. Born in Kent, Nicola spent 27 years in the South before relocating to the Midlands in 2001, where she pursued her post-graduate studies while raising her young family.

Having personally navigated the challenges of balancing family life, marriage, and a career, Nicola understands firsthand the importance of managing mental health while raising a family. Her passion lies in supporting parents to thrive, fostering a healthy family environment, and nurturing children's emotional development.

A keen exerciser and avid genealogy enthusiast, Nicola values the importance of making time for personal interests, which she believes is essential for self-care and life balance, something she encourages every parent to embrace. Through her work, Nicola blends practical strategies with deep emotional insight, empowering parents to reduce stress, prevent burnout, and cultivate a more harmonious home life.

In her book, Who Made You the Milk Police? - Managing Parental Burnout: 50 Tips for Stress-Free Parenting, Nicola shares compassionate, real-world advice, helping parents care for themselves while raising happy, emotionally resilient children. She believes self-care is not a luxury but a vital part of thriving as a parent.

PRIASE FOR NICOLA

The Empowered Parenting Programme has

been fantastic and has greatly helped us as a family. Completing the programme with my partner helped us both open up more about our experiences as children, the things we struggle with as parents, and the parents we want to be going forward. We have learnt so many strategies to help our children manage their emotions and behaviour and work as a team. I love that the programme helps you understand your child as well as yourself. Nicki is absolutely fantastic and so knowledgeable.

I recommend that anyone do this programme.

Lyndsey – Derby

This course has been a life changer. The best parenting course I have been on. It's delivered in a non-judgmental way and without blame. It looks at the root causes of why we parent in the way we do and how kids respond as a result. It teaches new ways to resolve current issues and helps you understand how and why they developed in the first place. Nicki understands so much, which helps you to feel accepted and that you are doing the best you can, which is everything when opening up.

Amazing, thank you so much! Nicki, you're amazing.

Anonymous - Derby

Being on this course has helped me understand that being the parent I want to be comes from understanding myself more. I thoroughly recommend this course.

Amanda - Derby

To explore further how you can work with Nicola simply scan the QR Code below.

Printed in Dunstable, United Kingdom